CBS NewsBreak 5

CBS ニュースブレイク 5

Nobuhiro Kumai Stephen Timson

StreamLine

Web 動画・音声ファイルのストリーミング再生について

CD マーク及び Web 動画マークがある箇所は、PC、スマートフォン、タブレット端末において、無料でストリーミング再生することができます。下記 URL よりご利用ください。再生手順や動作環境などは本書巻末の「Web 動画のご案内」をご覧ください。

http://st.seibido.co.jp

音声ファイルのダウンロードについて

CD マークがある箇所は、ダウンロードすることも可能です。下記 URL の書籍詳細ページにあるダウンロードアイコンをクリックしてください。

http://seibido.co.jp/ad603

はじめに

　このテキストはアメリカの３大ネットワークのひとつであるCBSの看板ニュース報道番組"CBS Evening News"と朝の情報番組"CBS This Morning"、そしてその日曜版の"CBS Sunday Morning"の中で取り上げられたニュースを収録したものです。これらの番組では時々刻々と変化する社会情勢や様々な出来事などが報道されますが、本テキストではそうした生々しいニュースというよりも、人々の日常の暮し、健康やライフスタイル、ハイテク、環境、経済、ポップカルチャー、エンターテインメントなどの話題を取り上げ、今アメリカで何が起こっているのか、何が問題になっているのか、人々の興味関心は何なのかなどについて紹介しています。個性豊かなアンカーや記者たちが様々な話題についてレポートしているため、英語を外国語として学んでいる学習者にとっても、たいへん興味深いものがあります。本書はその中から特に日本人英語学習者にとって身近で親しみやすく、アメリカ人の生活や文化を直接反映しているニュースを厳選しました。その中には現代日本の社会や事象が扱われている話題が含まれており、日本や日本文化が現在のアメリカ人にどのように受け止められているかを垣間見ることができます。

　IT技術の急速な進展のおかげで、本テキストのニュース素材がネットを通して、スマートフォンやコンピュータ上で簡単に視聴できるようになっています。ストリーミング形式での配信のため、手元の機器には保存することはできませんが、ネットにつながっていればいつでもどこからでも視聴することができます。学習する際には映像をヒントにしながら視聴しその内容を理解することが第１の目標となりますが、その内容を十分理解したあとでニュースの音声に合せて「シャドーイング」を行うことによって、英語の音声面の強化をはかることもめざしています。アンカーやレポーターたちは限られた時間内にできるだけ多くの情報を盛り込もうとしているため、１分間に150語から200語程度の速さで話しています。英語を外国語として学んでいる学習者がそれと同じように真似て復唱するのにはかなり無理がありますが、本テキストでは最新の話速変換技術を用いて、生の素材を生かしながらそのスピードを80％程度に遅くした音声や動画も併せて提供しています。ニュースに登場する人々の英語には生の感情がそのまま込められていますので、それをくりかえし練習することによってリスニング力を高めるとともに、英語特有の強弱のリズムやイントネーションをぜひ体感してください。また、各ユニットの最後にはニュースについて、「あなたはどう思いますか？あなたならどうしますか？」というように、話題を自分の立場に置き換えて考える活動が用意されています。多量のインプットに加えてこのように自分の考えをアウトプットすることによって、学習した言語項目を使いながら英語を身につけることができるようになっています。ニュースを理解するだけにとどまらず、様々な話題について自ら考え、それを英語で発信できる本物の英語力をぜひ身につけて下さい。

Nobuhiro Kumai & Stephen Timson

CONTENTS

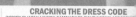

i川優実@#KuToo署名
ishikawa_yumi

CRACKING THE DRESS CODE
WOMEN IN JAPAN LAUNCH CAMPAIGN TO FIGHT WORKPLACE REQUIRE

She even answered somethin
I've always wondered about

1 Language Lessons

1 Before You Watch

Look at the title and photos and then answer the questions.

1. What do you think this boy is doing?

2. Why do you think he is wearing the message on the back of his vest jacket?

2 Word Match

Match each word or phrase with its definition below.

(   ) **1.** He **guarantee**d his team would get a victory in the championship game.

(   ) **2.** This new app provides perfect **translation**s in over 100 languages.

(   ) **3.** It will take me a while to get a **handle** on how this new phone works.

(   ) **4.** That historical building was **burned down** during the war, but it was rebuilt a few years later.

(   ) **5.** My sister **master**ed the guitar by taking free lessons online. She sounds like a pro!

(   ) **6.** Many Japanese companies **struggle**d to survive in the previous recession.

(   ) **7.** Most people think Mt. Fuji is dormant, but it actually is an active **volcano**.

(   ) **8.** I can't believe you finished everything so quickly! You're **awesome**!

---

a. to try very hard to do something when it is difficult

b. understanding or knowing something well

c. a mountain that sends out hot gas, rocks, ash, and lava (melted rock) into the air through a hole at the top or side

d. the process of changing words from one language into another

e. great, very impressive, or extremely good

f. to get the knowledge and skill that allows you to do, use, or understand (something) very well

g. to say that something will certainly happen with great confidence

h. destroyed by fire

---

3 Getting the Gist (First Viewing) [Time 02:03]

Watch the news and choose the right word or phrase in each statement.

1. Takuto has a great (command / communicator / speaker) of English.

2. Takuto mastered English by (taking private English lessons / using a language study program / visiting foreign countries).

4 Getting into Details (Second Viewing) [Time 02:03]   1-03~05

Watch or listen to the news again. Fill in the blanks and answer the questions.

[1-03]

Jeff Glor: We end here tonight with a trip to Japan. Ben Tracy **guarantee**s nothing will be lost in **translation**.

Takuto Kawakami: My name is Takuto Kawakami. I'm ten years old.

Ben Tracy: Takuto Kawakami has $_1$(   ).

5 *Takuto:* Where are you from? Why did you want to come to Japan? What is famous in Australia?

Tracy: But inside one of Japan's most famous gardens ...

Takuto: Can I talk a little about this garden?

10 *Tracy:* ... he also has $_2$(   ).

Takuto: This garden is called Korakuen. OK? Korakuen was made around 300 years ago. That is the Enyotei. And right next to the
15 Enyotei is the Kakumeikan. The Kakumeikan is a $_3$(   ), like a hotel.

Korakuen
岡山後楽園：日本庭園（大名庭園）で日本三名園の一つ

Enyotei
延養亭：藩主の静養や賓客の接待、藩校の儒学者の講義場として使われた後楽園の要の建物

Kakumeikan
鶴鳴館：来訪者をもてなす建物として使われた

Comprehension Check

1. [T / F] The Enyotei and Kakumeikan are located outside the Korakuen Garden.
2. [T / F] Takuto uses a translation app when he speaks to English speaking tourists who visit the Korakuen Garden.

[1-04]

Tracy: It's not just his **handle** on history that's unusual.

Takuto: These two buildings were **burned down** in World War II.

Tracy: In Japan, few people speak fluent English. Takuto **master**ed
20 it, passing a grueling English exam that $_4$(   ) Japanese adults fail.

not just ~
= not only ~

grueling
難しく過酷な

Takuto: And now I can speak English with you.

Tracy: You speak English very well.

25 *Takuto:* Really?

Tracy: Really well.

Takuto: Thank you.

Tracy: You're welcome. What's the $_5$(   ) about learning English?

30 *Takuto:* I **struggle**d with some words I didn't know.

Tracy: Like what?

Takuto: Like chrysanthemum.

Tracy: Chrysanthemum. Yeah, OK. That's a tough one.

chrysanthemum
菊

Comprehension Check

3. [T / F] Tracy thinks Takuto has a good understanding of the history of the Korakuen Garden.

4. [T / F] Most Japanese adults fail the English exam that Takuto passed.

[🎧 1-05]

Tracy: He $_6$(   ) of this in school.

35 *Takuto:* There's a programming [sic], Disney's World of English.

Program: Minnie is listening!

Tracy: He started using the Disney products when he was six months old. By four, he $_7$(   ).

Takuto: Most icy mountains are **volcano**es.

40 *Tracy:* Takuto proudly wears the names of the people he's met and by sharing his gift of language ...

Takuto: Thank you for listening.

programming
正しくは**program**
ディズニーキャラク
ターを使った英語学
習プログラム

9

Tracy: ... he's made their experience here a lot $_8$(   ).

| a lot ~ |
| とても〜（形容詞を修飾する） |

45　*Takuto:* Have a nice day and have a nice trip. And please ... please come back again. Bye!

Tracy: Ben Tracy, CBS News, Okayama, Japan.

Takuto: See you!

Glor: That kid is **awesome**.

Comprehension Check

5. [T / F]　Takuto learned English from a Disney program he watched at his school.
6. [T / F]　Foreign visitors enjoy their travel in Japan more because of Takuto's fluent language skills and historical explanations.

5　Summary

1-06

Fill in the blanks. The first two letters of each word are already given.

Takuto Kawakami is an unusual ten-year-old Japanese boy. He can speak $_1$(**fl**   ) English and passed a $_2$(**gr**   ) English exam that most Japanese adults fail. He started learning English from an English language learning $_3$(**pr**   ) called Disney's World of English when he was six months old. Takuto said the hardest part about mastering English was $_4$(**st**   ) with new words like chrysanthemum. He uses his language ability and $_5$(**ha**   ) on history to guide foreign visitors who visit Korakuen and some other famous buildings that were $_6$(**bu**   ) down in the Korakuen Garden during World War II. His English skills guarantee nothing is lost in $_7$(**tr**   ). The news reporter says Takuto helps make the experience of visiting a foreign country more familiar and enjoyable. The news anchor says Takuto's English language skills and knowledge of the history of the Korakuen Garden are $_8$(**aw**   ).

5

10

6 Conversation in Action

 1-07

Put the Japanese statements into English. Then listen to check your answers.

Emma: Hi Jacob, what's up?

Jacob: Hi. I'm ₁_____.

（この新しいアプリの使い方を理解するのに苦労しているところなんだ）

Emma: What's it for?

Jacob: Language translation. It says you ₂_____.

（どんな言語もマスターすることができる）

Emma: Sounds awesome! But that ₃_____.

（あなたが流暢になれるかは保証してくれないけどね）

Jacob: I know. But I'll give it a try.

Emma: Good luck!

7 Critical Thinking

Discuss the following questions with your partner or group. Give reasons to support your opinions.

Understanding the News

1. What does the phrase "lost in translation" mean?
2. Why does Ben Tracy guarantee nothing will be lost in translation?
3. What is special about Takuto Kawakami?

What Would You Do?

1. What are the advantages and disadvantages of learning a foreign language from an early age?
2. What advice would you give to a friend who is struggling to learn English?
3. Prepare a short report about a famous place or tourist spot in Japan and make a presentation to your group or class. Describe it and include background information about why it is famous, and things to see and do, etc.

2 U.S. Consumers Waste Food

Food / Consumerism

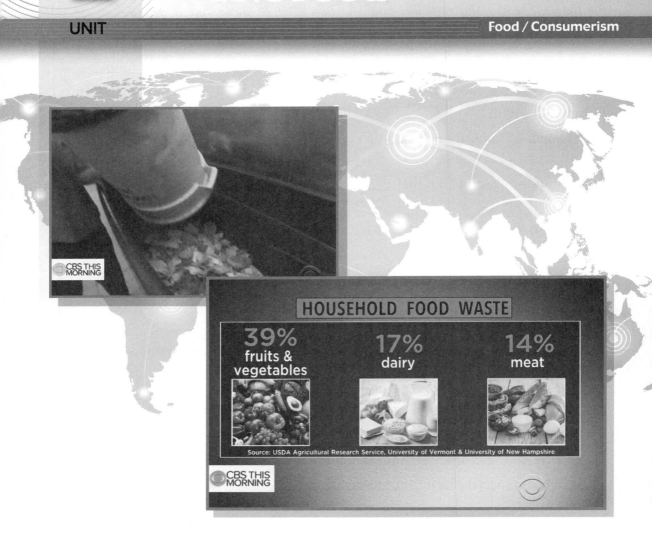

HOUSEHOLD FOOD WASTE

39% fruits & vegetables

17% dairy

14% meat

Source: USDA Agricultural Research Service, University of Vermont & University of New Hampshire

1 Before You Watch

Look at the title and photos and then answer the questions.

1. What do you usually do when produce in your kitchen looks spoiled or bad?

2. Do you avoid buying produce that doesn't look perfect or has an irregular shape?

2 Word Match

Match each word with its definition below.

(   ) **1.** A traditional Japanese **diet** of rice and fish is low in fat.

(   ) **2.** If you **consume** fewer calories than you need for energy, you will likely lose weight.

(   ) **3.** Nearly one in five **household**s in the U.S. lost work because of the pandemic.

(   ) **4.** When Tim was working on the **dairy** farm, he had to get up at five o'clock every morning to milk the cows.

(   ) **5.** The shop in our neighborhood sells only organic local **produce**.

(   ) **6.** If you have ugly, **bruised** apples that are still OK to eat, you can stew them or use them to make a pie.

(   ) **7.** Keep in mind that **spoiled** yogurt can cause food poisoning.

(   ) **8.** The articles on this webpage show how to **repurpose** old clothing.

---

a. milk or food made from milk (such as ice cream, cheese, or yogurt)

b. to change something so it can be used for a different purpose

c. to take in as food; to eat or drink something

d. having marks on fruits or vegetables caused by damage

e. the food that a person usually eats

f. fresh fruits or vegetables

g. the people in a family that are living together in one house

h. unable to be eaten because it has decayed or lost freshness especially because of being kept too long

---

3 Getting the Gist (First Viewing) [Time 01:42]

Watch the news and choose the right word or phrase in each statement.

1. The new study shows that U.S. consumers throw away nearly 150,000 tons of food (every day / every week / every month).

2. Understanding the difference between produce that is bruised and produce that is spoiled is important to (consume / decrease / reserve) food waste.

④ Getting into Details (Second Viewing) [Time 01:42] DVD 1-09, 10

Watch or listen to the news again. Fill in the blanks and answer the questions.

[🔊1-09]

Anne-Marie Green: New research suggests the healthier the **diet**, the more food waste there is likely to be. Here's Meg Oliver.

5 **Meg Oliver:** Stacy Moore visits the grocery store several times a week. As a private chef, she tries to ₁(   ).

private chef
パーティーなど個別
注文に応じて雇われ
る料理職人

Stacy Moore: People buy what they think they will **consume** and ₂(

10   ), they really don't.

Oliver: In fact, a new study shows U.S. consumers waste nearly 150,000 tons of food daily. That equals nearly a pound of food per person each day. The University of Vermont's Dr. Meredith Niles co-authored the research.

a pound
1 ポンド（約454グ
ラム）

15 **Dr. Meredith Niles:** In the bigger picture, it ... it's a waste of uh ... calories. It's a waste of potential environmental resources. But in our own

20 **household**s, it's also uh ... potentially a waste of our own ₃(   ) as well.

In the bigger picture
より大局的な見地か
ら見ると

potential
潜在的に有していて
将来的に使える見込
みのある

potentially
〜の可能性がある

Comprehension Check

1. [T / F] Stacy Moore says that people buy more food than they can eat.
2. [T / F] Each U.S. household wastes almost a pound of food per day.
3. [T / F] Buying more food than we can consume is a waste of calories and environmental and financial resources.

[🔊1-10]

Oliver: Researchers also found higher-quality diets were linked to ₄(   ) of waste. Fruits and vegetables

25 were thrown out the most – 39 percent of the total food wasted – followed by dairy and meat.

Oliver: Researchers say helping consumers understand the difference between produce that is bruised versus produce that is truly spoiled is important to

30   ₅(   ).

~ versus …
~対…

Dr. Niles: Just because a banana has a bruise on it, doesn't mean that we have to throw it away. And we could repurpose it. Maybe we don't wanna ₆(   ), but we could put it into a smoothie. We could blend it

35   up and make banana bread.

Oliver: Other suggestions include educating consumers on the proper way to store fresh fruits and vegetables so

40   ₇(   ), and revising sell-by dates for meat and dairy. Meg Oliver, CBS News, New York.

store
貯蔵する

revising sell-by dates
販売期限を見直すこと

BEST BY: FEB 09 88371 3 06:26 PROD OF USA

Comprehension Check

4. [T / F] The study found that dairy and meat products were wasted more than fruits and vegetables.

5. [T / F] Repurposing food such as bananas is a way to consume bruised produce that we might want to throw away.

6. [T / F] The study suggests that revising sell-by dates would help stop consumers from wasting food that is still good to consume.

Useful Tip

sell-by date：食品・製品などを公的に売ることができる最終日（販売期限、品質保持期限）
best by ~（best before ~）：~の時点より前が最もよい（おいしい）ことを表す賞味期限
  （その日を過ぎても食べる／飲むのはまだ安全である可能性あり）

5 Summary

 1-11

Fill in the blanks. The first two letters of each word are already given.

American households buy more food than they ₁(**co**   ).
In fact, almost a pound of food per person is thrown away each day. It
is not only a waste of calories and environmental resources, but also a
waste of ₂(**mo**   ). New studies show that higher-quality
₃(**di**   ) are linked to higher levels of food waste. Fruits and
vegetables are more likely to be thrown away than ₄(**da**   )
products and meat. Researchers say helping consumers understand the
difference between produce that is ₅(**br**   ) and produce that
is truly spoiled is important to reduce food waste. Another way to avoid
wastefulness is to ₆(**re**   ) the food we buy. So, instead of
throwing away fruit that is bruised, consumers can use it to make bread or
a smoothie. Learning proper ways to ₇(**st**   ) fresh fruits and
vegetables so they last longer, and ₈(**re**   ) sell-by dates for meat
and dairy products will also reduce waste.

6 Conversation in Action

1-12

Put the Japanese statements into English. Then listen to check your answers.

Jacob: The meat and dairy you got from the supermarket is great, but

1 _____. Look! It's all bruised!

（ その農作物が腐ってる ）

Emma: Wait! Don't throw it out! I can ₂_____.

（ それを本来の目的を変えてパイやパンにする ）

Jacob: So it's still safe to consume?

Emma: Of course! We'll not only save money and have a healthy diet, but ₃_____

_____.

（ 食べ物を無駄にすることも避けることになるわ ）

7 Conversation in Action 🏔 CHALLENGE

Use the vocabulary and phrases you learned in Word Match and the news report scripts to make a short conversation with your partner. Then practice your conversation with your partner or group.

_____: _____
(Name)

_____: _____
(Name)

_____: _____
(Name)

_____: _____
(Name)

8 Critical Thinking

Discuss the following questions with your partner or group. Give reasons to support your opinions.

Understanding the News

1. What does the new study report about U.S. consumers?
2. What do researchers say is important for consumers to know about produce in order to avoid food waste?
3. What are some ways consumers can avoid wasting food?
4. What does "sell-by date" mean?

What Would You Do?

1. What are some ways people waste food?
2. How can people avoid wasting food?
3. What are some ways you can repurpose foods and other products? Share your ideas with your partner, group, or class.
4. Hoarding, or buying large quantities of food and other products to use later, has become a serious problem recently, especially during national emergencies. Give some examples and reasons for hoarding.

3 Keeping eSports Athletes in the Game

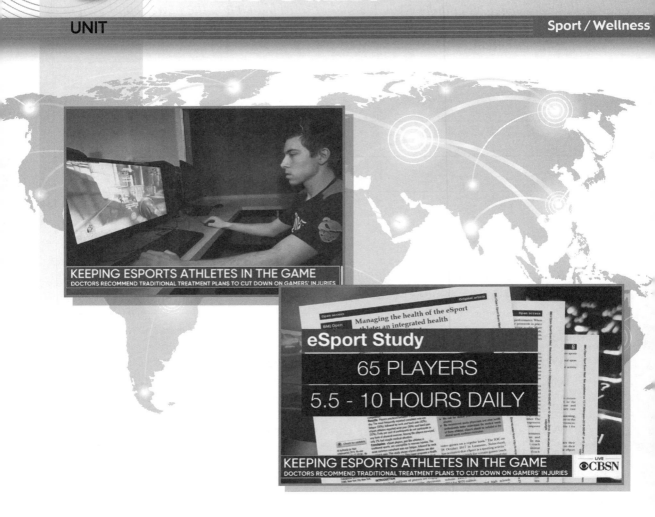

1 Before You Watch

Look at the title and photos and then answer the questions.

1. What is an eSport?

2. What do you think might happen to you if you play video games for a long time?

2 Word Match

Match each word or phrase with its definition below.

(   ) **1.** My favorite player left the game due to a serious **injury**.

(   ) **2.** Playing on the **varsity** football team in college was hard work, but a lot of fun.

(   ) **3.** The infectious viral disease began to **take a toll** among the people living in that area.

(   ) **4.** Finding a new coach for our team was quite a **draining** experience.

(   ) **5.** Good **posture** is important when using a computer.

(   ) **6.** She broke down from **fatigue** after working too hard.

(   ) **7.** I can't sleep very well lately. I might be suffering from **insomnia**.

(   ) **8.** I couldn't **suppress** my anger when I heard about the new tax.

---

a. extreme tiredness resulting from mental or physical activity or illness

b. the primary or best team of a college or high school in sports competitions

c. the condition of not being able to sleep

d. to cause harm or damage, or have a serious, bad effect on someone or something

e. to stop the growth or development of something

f. making you weaker; causing you to lose strength and energy

g. physical harm or damage done to a person or a part of their body

h. the position that your body is in when you sit, stand, or walk

---

3 Getting the Gist (First Viewing) [Time 02:04]

Watch the news and choose the right word in each statement.

1. Researchers (advise / insist / require) that schools have prevention and treatment plans for eSport injuries, just like they do for traditional sports.

2. The most commonly reported complaints by eSport athletes are (agreed / connected / matched) to eye strain and fatigue.

4 **Getting into Details (Second Viewing)** [Time 02:04]   1-14~16

Watch or listen to the news again. Fill in the blanks and answer the questions.

[1-14]

Reena Ninan: While eSports become more popular, **injuri**es related to gaming are ₁(   ), too. Tom Hanson shows us what doctors are recommending.

Tom Hanson: Ryan Harran and Daniel Singh have taken their
5   ₂(   ) to the collegiate level. At the New York Institute of Technology, they play **varsity** eSports for the CyBears.

Ryan Harran: Some days I won't play at all, just 'cause of school
10   and work. But when I do play, it could be from anywhere from like, three hours to like, six hours.

Some days
～する日もある

Comprehension Check

1. **[T / F]** As eSports become more popular, the rate of player injuries has increased.
2. **[T / F]** Ryan Harran and Daniel Singh play eSports for their high school varsity team.
3. **[T / F]** Ryan plays eSports every day even though he is busy studying and working.

[1-15]

Hanson: And they say like other sports, that practice **take**s **a toll**.

15 **Daniel Singh:** It is pretty mentally **draining**. There's definitely eye strain, uh, from just, you know, ₃(   ).

eye strain
目の疲れ、眼精疲労

Hanson: New research in the British Journal of Medicine looked at 65 college eSport
20   athletes, and found they played about ₄(
) to ten hours a day, with many reporting

25 overuse injuries, including hand, wrist, neck, and back pain.

overuse ~
使いすぎによる～

Dr. Hallie Zwibel (the NYIT Center for Sports Medicine): Poor **posture** can produce exponential forces on your neck, back, shoulder.

exponential
（指数関数的に）
急激な

30 Eye **fatigue** is the most commonly reported complaint from these pixelate [sic] images that you see when you are $_5$(

complaint
（患者が訴える）
病状、症状
pixelate(d) images
画素で構成された映像（画素が目立ちきれいに見えない）

). They're making 500 action moves per minute. So

35 there's a lot of high-speed thinking. I think that fatigues the eyes even further.

Comprehension Check

4. [T / F] eSport athletes say playing eSports is just as physically tiring as other sports.

5. [T / F] New research in the British Journal of Medicine reported that college eSport athletes played ten hours every five days.

6. [T / F] Poor posture while playing eSports produces exponential forces on your neck and other parts of your body.

[🎧 1-16]

Hanson: Study author, Dr. Hallie Zwibel says players also report **insomnia**, because the $_6$(   ) from screens can **suppress** the sleep hormone, melatonin.

melatonin
メラトニン（入眠を助ける効果があるホルモン）

40 So far more than 80 colleges and universities in the U.S. have varsity eSport teams. Researchers stress schools $_7$(   )

D WESTBURY, NY

TOM HANSON
S CBS NEWS | = THOMASRHANSON

stress
強調する
prevention and treatment plans
防止と治療の計画

45 prevention and treatment plans for injuries just as they do with traditional athletes.

Nutritional exercise regimens
栄養・運動管理療法

Dr. Zwibel: Nutritional exercise regimens, stretches, especially

50 stretches of the eyes to prevent eye fatigue during game play.

Hanson: Daniel says he keeps all of that in mind to be his best on game day.

Singh: You try to $_8$( )

55 of your posture, try to roll your shoulders back, keep a straight back.

Hanson: He also tries to work some exercise into his week when he's offline. Tom Hanson, CBS News, Old (Westbury,

60 New York.)

work some exercise into his week
いくらかの運動を一週間の間に組み込む

Comprehension Check

7. **[T / F]** People who play eSports cannot focus on their gaming because the blue light from their screens makes them sleepy.

8. **[T / F]** Researchers say that since the number of eSport teams in colleges and universities is growing, they must have the same support programs that prevent and treat injuries as they do with other sports and athletes.

9. **[T / F]** Nutritional exercise regimens and special eye exercises are important to prevent eye fatigue on days when eSport athletes play.

5 Summary

 1-17

Fill in the blanks. The first two letters of each word are already given.

An eSport, or electronic sport, is a competitive sport using video games. eSports are becoming more and more popular on college campuses. Playing eSports takes a $_1$(**to**   ) on the body. Like athletes in other sports, eSport players get injured, and these $_2$(**in**   ) are increasing. Ryan Harran and Daniel Singh play eSports for their college $_3$(**va**   ) 5 team. Ryan says that playing a game can take from three to six hours. Practicing takes a lot of time, too. Poor $_4$(**po**   ) when playing can produce exponential forces on your neck, back, and shoulders. Playing an eSport is also mentally $_5$(**dr**   ) and causes eye $_6$(**fa**   ). The blue light from computer screens can cause $_7$(**in**   ) 10 because it suppresses the sleep hormone, melatonin. Doctors recommend that colleges provide prevention and treatment plans, such as nutritional exercise $_8$(**re**   ) , and muscle and eye stretches.

6 Conversation in Action

 1-18

Put the Japanese statements into English. Then listen to check your answers.

Emma: Hey Jacob, what's with the weird faces?

Jacob: Hey, Emma. I'm doing eye stretches and some other exercise regimens.

Emma: What for?

Jacob: I'm on the varsity eSports team. I $_1$_____
_____. (他のスポーツで時々選手たちがするようなけがをしたくないんだよ)

Emma: *For real?* I've never thought of gaming as a sport before. That is so cool. I guess playing eSports $_2$_____, and it must be mentally draining, too.   (とても体に負担をかける)

Jacob: That's right. $_3$_____, and the blue light from screens can cause insomnia, so I've got to stay in shape. (姿勢が悪いと背中を痛めることがある)

Emma: Playing eSports is harder than I thought. Go CyBears!

> **Word Help** *For real?:* used in questions to express surprise or to question the truth about something. *Example:* "I just got a summer internship in Paris." "For real?"

7 Conversation in Action  CHALLENGE

Use the vocabulary and phrases you learned in Word Match and the news report scripts to make a short conversation with your partner. Then practice your conversation with your partner or group.

_____: _____
(Name)

_____: _____
(Name)

_____: _____
(Name)

_____: _____
(Name)

8 Critical Thinking

Discuss the following questions with your partner or group. Give reasons to support your opinions.

Understanding the News

1. What is the most common injury related to eSports?
2. What does Daniel Singh do to prevent gaming injuries?
3. What do researchers and doctors recommend that colleges and players do to treat and prevent eSports injuries?

What Would You Do?

1. Are you a gamer, or do you play eSports? Why?/Why not? If yes, what games do you play, and how often do you play?
2. Do you think playing video games is good or bad for you?
3. Does your college or university have an eSport club or team? Would you be interested in forming or joining one? Why?/ Why not?
4. Do you ever get injuries from gaming? What advice for avoiding gaming injuries would you give to your friends?

4 Adulting Classes for Millennials

CBS THIS MORNING

LIVING AT HOME
18-34 YEAR OLDS

34%

26%

2015

2005

CBS THIS MORNING

The Changing Fr... of Your... ...raphics

1 Before You Watch

Look at the title and photos and then answer the questions.

1. What do you think the title of this news report means?

2. What does the chart in the photo above show about people aged 18-34 years old?

Adulting Classes Learn Life Skills!

2 Word Match

Match each word or phrase with its definition below.

(   ) **1. Millennials** are people who were born or brought up during the age of digital technology.

(   ) **2.** I was just appointed manager of our Mexico branch, so I signed up for a **crash course** in Spanish.

(   ) **3.** Many English conversation schools in Japan offer language study courses **geared toward** children.

(   ) **4.** That company **launch**ed a new co-working space business in Tokyo last month.

(   ) **5.** There has been a long economic **conflict** between those two countries.

(   ) **6.** Some people refer to their **spouse** as "my better half."

(   ) **7.** I spent the last three days **figur**ing **out** the new IT system at work.

(   ) **8.** I missed a week of classes, so I have to **catch up** now.

---

a. to start selling a new product or service to the public

b. designed or organized to achieve a particular purpose, or to be suitable for a particular group of people

c. a husband or wife

d. to be able to understand something or to solve a problem

e. people who belong to the generation who were born between 1981 and 1996

f. to try to reach the same standard or level as someone else because you have fallen behind

g. a class in which you are taught a lot about a subject in a short time

h. a strong disagreement between people, groups, etc.

---

3 Getting the Gist (First Viewing) [Time 02:18]

Watch the news and choose the right word in each statement.

1. Many millennial adults feel that they haven't learned much about basic (life / professional / study) skills.

2. Because many young adults still live with their (friends / parents / partners), they tend to delay important life events, like marriage and having children.

4 **Getting into Details (Second Viewing)** [Time 02:18] WEB動画 🖥 DVD CD 1-20~22

Watch or listen to the news again. Fill in the blanks and answer the questions.

[CD 1-20]

Brook Silva-Braga: I'm Brook Silva-Braga with a look beyond this morning's headlines. **Millennial**s lacking life skills, like cooking, budgeting, or time-management. Well, they're now signing up for classes designed to teach them those basics. Laura Podesta tells us about the **crash course** in adulting.

Kim Calichio (Chef): Um, I'm gonna show you guys ₁(
).

Laura Podesta: At this cooking class in Queens, New York, 29-year-old Elena Toumaras says she's finally learning skills she wishes she'd been taught years ago.

Elena Toumaras: I don't know, I was so used to, like when I was living at home, my mom always cooking. And me, just ₂(
). And now that I'm on my own ... still kind of struggling with it.

headlines	トップニュース
budgeting	家計・生活費の管理
you guys	皆さんに
now that ~	（もう）今は～なので

Comprehension Check

1. **[T / F]** Adulting classes are for millennials who want to learn how to get a better job or develop their careers.
2. **[T / F]** Elena feels she didn't learn enough about cooking and other important life skills when she was younger.

[CD 1-21]

Podesta: She's not alone. The number of classes **geared toward** teaching adults ₃(
) is growing.

Podesta: Rachel Flehinger co-founded the aptly named Adulting
25 School in Portland, Maine. This month, she's **launch**ing
online classes geared toward millennials anywhere
who want to know how to sew a button, understand
modern art, or tell someone they love them.

Rachel Flehinger: How to have a
30 relationship, how to talk
to somebody, **conflict**
resolution — how not to
fight.

Podesta: Experts say millennials $_4($) because many
35 haven't left childhood homes. The U.S. Census Bureau
says in 2015, 34 percent of Americans between 18 and
34 still lived $_5($). That's compared
to just 26 percent in 2005.

Jonathan Vespa (Demographer): It is more
40 common than uh … living
with roommates and more
common than living with a
spouse.

Podesta: That translates into young adults $_6($),
45 having children later, and ultimately **figur**ing **out**
those crucial life skills later, too.

co-founded
共同で設立した

aptly named
ぴったりな名前の

resolution
解決すること

U.S. Census
Bureau
米国国勢調査局

That's compared
to ~
それに比べて…年で
は~である

translates into ~
（結果として）~
になる
ultimately
最終的には

---

3. [T / F] Conflict resolution courses teach millennials how to find a peaceful way to
settle a problem or disagreement.

4. [T / F] The percentage of millennials living with a parent has slowly decreased
since 2005.

5. [T / F] Data shows that millennials living with a parent is now more common than
those living with roommates or a spouse.

6. [T / F] Experts say living with a parent is a reason why young adults are getting
married and having children later.

[CD 1-22]

Podesta: What's the most ₇(   ) that someone in their late 20s has come to you and asked?

Calichio: I'm always surprised about
50 uh … people not knowing what I think are the simple things, in terms of knife skills, or flavors that may go together …

in terms of ~
~に関して、~と言う点で

55 *Podesta:* Chef Kim Calichio says she's happy to keep teaching classes to help millennials **catch up** in the kitchen. Better ₈(   ). Laura Podesta, CBS News, Queens, New York.

Comprehension Check

7. [T / F] Kim says she's surprised that millennials don't even know simple cooking skills.
8. [T / F] Kim enjoys teaching cooking to those who want to learn basic cooking skills.

5 Summary

 1-23

Fill in the blanks. The first two letters of each word are already given.

Laura Podesta reports about a ₁(**cr**   ) course in adulting. Rachel Flehinger co-founded the Adulting School in Portland, Maine to help people between the ages of 18 to 34 learn how to be adults. ₂(**Mi**   ) adults are going back to school and pursuing courses ₃(**ge**   ) toward essential life skills like cooking, sewing, understanding modern art, developing personal relationships, and ₄(**co**   ) resolution. Experts say millennials are behind in these skills because one-third of them still live with their parents. That's more common than living with roommates or a ₅(**sp**   ). So they haven't learned to ₆(**fi**   ) out these things by themselves. Millennials not only marry and have children later, but also learn ₇(**cr**   ) life skills later, too. Chef Kim Calichio says she is most surprised when she is asked what she thinks are simple things, such as knife skills or mixing the right food flavors together. She's happy to teach classes to help millennials ₈(**ca**   ) up in the kitchen.

5

10

6 Conversation in Action

1-24

Put the Japanese statements into English. Then listen to check your answers.

Emma: I can't ₁_____ about a problem with my boss.
（どうしたらよいかわからない）

Jacob: You should take an adulting class.

Emma: Those classes are ₂_____, right?
（ミレニアル世代向けよね）

Jacob: Yeah. They teach you ₃_____
_____, personal relationships, how to pursue a goal, even cooking.（あなたの上司や配偶者との対立を解決することのような極めて重要な人生のスキル）

Emma: Wow, I'd really like to learn stuff like that.

Jacob: Me, too. Let's take a class together.

7 Conversation in Action ⟨△ CHALLENGE⟩

Use the vocabulary and phrases you learned in Word Match and the news report scripts to make a short conversation with your partner. Then practice your conversation with your partner or group.

_____: _____
(Name)

_____: _____
(Name)

_____: _____
(Name)

_____: _____
(Name)

8 Critical Thinking

Discuss the following questions with your partner or group. Give reasons to support your opinions.

Understanding the News

1. What is an adulting class?

2. What can you learn in an adulting class? Give some examples.

3. Why do millennials need an adulting class?

What Would You Do?

1. Do you think adulting classes are a good idea? Why?/Why not?

2. Do you think you know enough essential life skills?

3. Would you take an adulting class? Why?/Why not? If yes, what would you like to learn?

5 Is Your Bottled Water Safe?

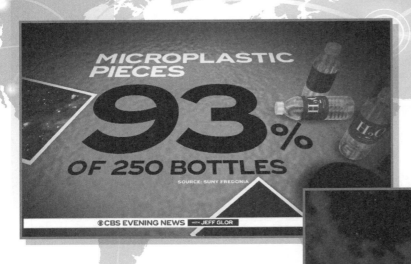

1 Before You Watch

Look at the title and photos and then answer the questions.

1. How often do you drink bottled water?

2. Why do you think people drink bottled water?

2 Word Match

Match each word or phrase with its definition below.

(   ) **1.** Microplastics are tiny plastic **particle**s and are found almost everywhere.

(   ) **2.** The anti-virus scan results **identifi**ed the cause of the computer problem.

(   ) **3.** The new study says people worldwide might be **ingest**ing five grams of microplastics every week.

(   ) **4.** Many advocacy groups are **push**ing **back** against online hate speech and systemic racism.

(   ) **5.** All the things he said about seeing ghosts in the house **scare**d me.

(   ) **6.** Research has **confirm**ed that the risk of having an accident in the home is higher for older people.

(   ) **7.** As long as you work here, you'll have to **adhere to** company rules and regulations.

(   ) **8.** There are three main types of **contamination**: solid particle, air and water.

---

a. to take food or drink into the body

b. to oppose or resist a plan, an idea, or a change

c. to say or show that something is definitely true or correct, especially by providing evidence

d. the process of making something dirty or no longer pure by adding something dangerous

e. a very small piece of something

f. to follow a particular rule, law, or agreement

g. to recognize something and understand exactly what it is

h. to make someone become afraid or worried

---

3 Getting the Gist (First Viewing) [Time 01:55]

Watch the news and choose the right word or phrase in each statement.

1. In a new study, tiny pieces of plastics were found in (a few / half of / most) of the bottles of water that researchers tested.

2. Many people (doubt / don't know / know) that there may be microplastics in the bottles of water they drink every day.

4 Getting into Details (Second Viewing) [Time 01:55]   1-26~28

Watch or listen to the news again. Fill in the blanks and answer the questions.

[🎧 1-26]

Jeff Glor: A new study out today is shaking up a [sic] bottled water business. It found plastic **particle**s floating
5 in some of the most popular brands. Now the World Health Organization is looking into it. Here's Anna Werner.

shaking up 揺るがして・衝撃を与えて

Anna Werner: Scientists found tiny pieces of plastic in more than 90
10 percent of the 250 bottles of water they tested. Virtually all were ₁( ). The largest, about the width of a human hair. The study **identifi**ed some of the plastic as polypropylene, the same type of plastic used in ₂( ).

Virtually 実質的には（～と言っていいくらい）

polypropylene ポリプロピレン

15 To find those tiny pieces, scientists used a special dye that ₃( ). Those lighter bits you see floating, they
20 say, that's the plastic.

dye 染料

Comprehension Check

1. [T / F] Scientists found human hair in over 90 percent of the water bottles they tested.
2. [T / F] Polypropylene is the same type of plastic used to make water bottles.
3. [T / F] Scientists used a special dye to find tiny pieces of plastic inside 250 bottles of water.

[🎧 1-27]

Werner: Professor Sherri Mason ran the test commissioned by nonprofit journalism group, Orb Media.

commissioned by ~ ～から委託された

Prof. Sherri Mason: If you're drinking only bottled water and you do this every day, over, you

25   know, a year, you know, you're literally talking $_4($ $)$ of plastic that you're **ingest**ing just simply from

30   the bottled water that you're drinking.

Werner: The water came from 11 different brands in nine countries. And the report says the amount of particles varied from bottle to bottle, even among packs from the same brand. But the bottled water contained $_5($

35            $)$ plastic as in a previous study of tap water.

are literally
talking ~
文字通り〜もの…を
〜しているというこ
とになるのです（数
を強調）

varied from
bottle to bottle
ボトルによって異な
っていた
packs
パック包装された
商品
tap water 水道水

Comprehension Check

4. [T / F] The water bottle study was commissioned by the World Health Organization.

5. [T / F] The water was tested by a professor doing research for a nonprofit journalism organization.

6. [T / F] Scientists found the same amount of microplastic particles in both bottled and tap water.

[🎧1-28]

Werner: The bottled water industry group is **push**ing **back**, saying the report is $_6($ $)$ sound science and unnecessarily **scare**s consumers. Some of the companies, including Nestlé Waters, said they do

40   their own tests and cannot **confirm** the findings here. All say they **adhere to** strict safety standards. But, Jeff, some companies confirmed

45   they are aware of the issue of microplastic **contamination**, uh, which is something that I think consumers were $_7($ $)$, at

sound science
健全な（論理的に正
しい）科学

findings
調査結果

least most people.

Glor: Yeah, it sure makes $_8$(   ). All right,

50   Anna, thank you very much.

Comprehension Check

7. [T / F] The bottled water industry does not support the study results and thinks it is not helpful for consumers.

8. [T / F] The reporter says most people are not aware that the bottled water they drink contains microplastic particles.

5 Summary   1-29

Fill in the blanks. The first two letters of each word are already given.

A new study commissioned by Orb Media found microplastic $_1$(**co**   ) in bottled drinking water. Scientists used a special dye to $_2$(**id**   ) plastic in the water. Some of the plastic was polypropylene, the same type of plastic used to make bottle caps. That means if you drink only bottled water, you're literally $_3$(**in**   ) thousands of plastic $_4$(**pa**   ) a year! The water came from 11 different brands in nine countries. The amount of particles varied from bottle to bottle, even among bottles from the same brand. And bottled water contained $_5$ (**tw**   ) as much plastic as in a previous study of tap water. The bottled water industry is $_6$(**pu**   ) back, saying they cannot $_7$(**co**   ) the findings because the report is not based on sound science. They say it just frightens consumers and that they $_8$(**ad**   ) to strict safety standards. Though bottled water makers are aware of this issue, most people are not.

5

10

Useful Tip

「知覚動詞 + 名詞 + ~ing 形」の構造と意味

「～が見える・聞こえる・感じられる」などを表す**知覚動詞** (see, hear, feel) や「～がわかる」を表す動詞 (find) の場合、その目的語となる「名詞」と「~ing 形」の間に、**意味上の主述関係**、つまり、主語と述語の関係が成り立っています。このような英文を理解する際には、このことを意識して意味をとらえるようにしましょう。

＜本文 3~6 行目＞

It <u>found</u> plastic particles <u>floating</u> ~ .
　　　　（意味上の）主語　　 述語

ここでは <u>floating</u> ～ は前の名詞を修飾しているのではなく、plastic particles と floating の間には**意味上、主語と述語の関係**が成り立っています。つまり、「It ＝ The new study」なので、「その新しい研究では、＜プラスチックの小片（意味上の主語）**が**～に浮かん**でいる**（意味上の述語）＞ことがわかった」ということになります。
本文 18 ~ 20 行目の <u>Those lighter bits</u> <u>you</u> <u>see</u> <u>floating</u>, they say, that's the plastic. の文も同様に考えてみましょう。

6 Conversation in Action

 1-30

Put the Japanese statements into English. Then listen to check your answers.

Emma: Did you hear about the microplastic contamination in bottled water?

Jacob: Yeah. They ₁_____ in the water.
（プラスチックを同定するのに特別な染料を使ったんだよね）

Emma: That means you're literally ₂_____ a year!
（何千ものプラスチックのかけらを体内に取り込んでいる）

Jacob: *Whoa*! I bet the bottled water companies are pushing back, right?

Emma: Yeah! They say they ₃_____
because they're not based on sound science. （その調査結果を確かめることができない）

Jacob: Well, I'm switching to tap water just in case.

Word Help *Whoa:* used to express surprise, interest, or alarm, or to command attention. *Example:* "Whoa, that's huge!"

7 Conversation in Action  CHALLENGE

Use the vocabulary and phrases you learned in Word Match and the news report scripts to make a short conversation with your partner. Then practice your conversation with your partner or group.

_____: _____
(Name)

_____: _____
(Name)

_____: _____
(Name)

_____: _____
(Name)

8 Critical Thinking

Discuss the following questions with your partner or group. Give reasons to support your opinions.

Understanding the News

1. Describe the new study and its findings.
2. What effect does drinking only bottled water have on people who drink it daily?
3. How is the water bottle industry pushing back?

What Would You Do?

1. Are you concerned about the discovery of plastic in bottled water?
2. Bottled water is often advertised as being cleaner than tap water. Do you agree? Why? / Why not?
3. How can you avoid microplastic contamination in bottled water?

6 Sleepless in Japan

1 Before You Watch

Look at the title and photos and then answer the questions.

1. How many hours do you usually sleep?

2. What happens to you when you don't get enough
    sleep?

2 Word Match

Match each word or phrase with its definition below.

(   ) **1.** Many parents are **sacrific**ing to pay for their children's college tuition.

(   ) **2.** Researchers are attempting to develop better treatments for **chronic** diseases like diabetes and cancer.

(   ) **3.** Sleep **deprivation** has a very negative effect on health and productivity.

(   ) **4.** The novel coronavirus has **afflict**ed millions of people all over the world.

(   ) **5.** The coach **urge**d us to do some physical exercise at home since our practices have been cancelled.

(   ) **6.** She's working at a law **firm** based in London.

(   ) **7.** You can get the most out of your vacation if you just **unplug** and communicate in person rather than online.

(   ) **8.** Some politicians seem to be more **concerned with** power and control than with people's well-being and happiness.

---

a. the state of not having something that people need

b. to advise someone very strongly about what they should do

c. to refrain from using digital or electronic devices or social media for a period of time

d. serious and lasting for a long time

e. a business or company

f. to give up (something that you want to keep) especially in order to get or do something else or to help someone

g. to cause pain or suffering (to someone or something)

h. having an interest in something

---

3 Getting the Gist (First Viewing) [Time 02:45]

Watch the news and choose the right word in each statement.

1. Chronic sleep deprivation has negative (causes / effects / reports) on the health and job performance of both Americans and Japanese.

2. Professor Nishino says that the quality of sleep is just as (essential / frequent serious) as the quantity.

4 Getting into Details (Second Viewing) [Time 02:45] 1-32~34

Watch or listen to the news again. Fill in the blanks and answer the questions.

[🎧1-32]

Anne-Marie Green: And New York may be the city that never sleeps. But Japan may be the actual place suffering from sleeplessness. Workers there are **sacrific**ing sleep in order to work harder. Lucy Craft has more from Tokyo.

5 *Lucy Craft:* In Japan, it's socially acceptable to grab 40 winks just about anywhere – on a train, over coffee, even in Parliament. And yes, that is Prime Minister Abe.

Snoozing in public is ₁( ) it even has a name:
10 *inemuri*, or sleeping on duty.

But among a growing number of Japanese, the alarm has gone off about the wisdom of sacrificing ₂( ).

the city that never sleeps
ニューヨーク市のニックネーム

grab 40 winks
うたた寝［昼寝］をする

Parliament
国会

the alarm has gone off
警鐘が鳴った

the wisdom of ~
～するのが賢明であること

Comprehension Check

1. [T / F] In Japanese culture, sleeping anywhere, like on a train, in cafés, or other public places is unusual and unacceptable.
2. [T / F] *Inemuri* means snoozing when you should be working or paying attention.
3. [T / F] More and more Japanese are starting to realize the effects of working hard without getting enough sleep.

[🎧1-33]

15 *Craft:* Stanford University professor Seiji Nishino, who runs the school's Sleep and Circadian Neurobiology Lab, says **chronic** sleep **deprivation afflict**s Americans and Japanese alike.

Craft: So we're ₃( ).

20 *Prof. Nishino:* Too late, yes. That's not only for the adults … uh …

Sleep and Circadian Neurobiology Lab
睡眠・生体リズム研究所

also for the kids ... uh ... same tendency.

25 *Craft:* Worried about the impact of sleeplessness on productivity, a few Japanese companies now **urge** their employees to take power naps — on the job. At least one **firm** $_4$( ) to get enough sleep at night, and Japanese cities now feature "napping cafés."

30 While Japan ranked dead last among 100 countries in hours slept, the U.S. Centers for Disease Control says one-third of Americans are not getting the recommended minimum of $_5$( ).

35 The CDC says our irregular, 24-7, always-on lifestyles put us at risk for obesity, cancer, dementia, and shortened lifespan, not to mention hampering job performance.

power nap
30分以下の短い仮眠

feature ~
特徴として~を持つ

ranked dead last
最下位だった

Centers for Disease Control
《米》疾病対策センター

obesity
（病的な）肥満

dementia
認知症

not to mention ~
~は言うまでもなく

hampering ~
~を妨げること

Comprehension Check

4. [T / F] Prof. Nishino says not only adults but also children have a tendency to go to bed later at night.
5. [T / F] A small number of Japanese firms are encouraging their employees to take power naps before coming to work.
6. [T / F] Less than one-third of Americans are getting the recommended minimum of seven hours of sleep a night.
7. [T / F] The CDC says today's modern and always changing way of living puts people at risk for diseases and has a negative effect on their lifespan and job performance.

[🎧 1-34]

40 *Craft:* Author of a comic book of sleep tips, Nishino advises CEOs and sumo wrestlers alike $_6$( ) and **unplug**, well before hitting the hay.

CEO
chief executive officer（最高経営責任者）

hitting the hay
床につく、寝ること

45 ***Craft:*** You and other researchers have also said that even if you get seven hours or eight hours ...

Prof. Nishino: Yes.

Craft: ... of sleep, quantity $_7($). Why is that?

50 ***Prof. Nishino:*** Most of the people [sic] [are] **concerned** [**with**] length of sleep, but quality is also important.

Craft: Quality shut-eye starts with a regular pre-sleep routine, like an evening stroll or reading a book, and not checking email. Sleep, Nishino warns, can be our best friend, or
55 $_8($). Lucy Craft, CBS News, Tokyo.

shut-eye
眠り
pre-sleep routine
床につく前に習慣的
にする行動
evening stroll
夜の散歩

Comprehension Check

8. [T / F] Prof. Nishino advises people to relax and not use any electronic devices before going to bed.
9. [T / F] The kind of sleep you get is less important than the amount.
10. [T / F] Changing your pre-sleep routine regularly is a good way to get quality sleep.

5 Summary

 CD 1-35

Fill in the blanks. The first two letters of each word are already given.

Japanese workers are not getting enough $_1$(**sl**   ). *Inemuri*, or snoozing in public, is very common. Stanford University professor Seiji Nishino says both adults and children have a tendency to $_2$(**st**   ) up too late because of their irregular 24-7 lifestyles. Japan ranked dead last among 100 countries in hours slept. The U.S. Centers for Disease Control says $_3$(**on   -th**   ) of Americans are not getting the recommended minimum of seven hours of sleep a night. That can cause chronic sleep $_4$(**de**   ). Lack of sleep also puts us at $_5$(**ri**   ) for obesity, cancer, dementia, a shortened lifespan, and affects job $_6$(**pe**   ) and productivity. A few Japanese firms encourage their employees to take a power nap during work hours, and even pay them to sleep more. However, the quantity of sleep does not equal $_7$(**qu**   ). Professor Nishino recommends slowing down and $_8$(**un**   ) from electronic devices, and taking a walk or reading before going to sleep.

5

10

15

6 Conversation in Action

CD 1-36

Put the Japanese statements into English. Then listen to check your answers.

Emma: Hey, Jacob! Wake up ... Wake up!

Jacob: Eh? What? What happened?

Emma: You were snoozing in class again.

Jacob: Oh, *my bad*. I think I get enough sleep at night. But I still feel tired during the day. Maybe $_1$_____.

(寝不足かも)

Emma: *For sure*! You were *out like a light*! And remember, $_2$_____
_____. (睡眠の量は質と同じじゃないのよ)

Jacob: You're right. I don't want to $_3$_____
_____.

(自分自身を病気になる危険にさらしたり、授業の単位を落としたりする)

I need a pre-sleep routine and … to unplug from my devices.

Emma: And stop taking power naps in class!

> **Word Help** *my bad: to admit that you are wrong or that something is your fault.
> >   *Example:* "Sorry I'm late. It's my bad."
> > *For sure: used to show strong agreement with a statement.
> >   *Example:* "Don't forget to wear a mask on the airplane." "For Sure!"
> > *out like a light: to fall asleep very quickly or immediately.
> >   *Example:* As soon as my head touched the pillow, I was out like a light.

7 Critical Thinking

Discuss the following questions with your partner or group. Give reasons to support your opinions.

Understanding the News

1. What is sleep deprivation and what is the cause?

2. What are some harmful effects of sleep deprivation?

3. What are a few Japanese companies doing to make sure their employees get enough sleep?

What Would You Do?

1. Do you ever take power naps or snooze on duty (*inemuri*)? When, and Why?

2. Do you have a regular pre-sleep routine? Describe it. Discuss your routine with your partner or group.

3. What are some things you can do to improve the quantity and quality of your sleep? Discuss your answer with your partner or group.

7 Alarming New Climate Report

NEGATIVE EFFECTS ON OCEANS
FROM CLIMATE CHANGE:
SEVERE STORMS

BREAKING NEWS
ALARMING NEW CLIMATE REPORT
100+ SCIENTISTS SAY OCEANS RISING AT DEVASTATING RATE

① Before You Watch

Look at the title and photos and then answer the questions.

1. Why do you think this news report is alarming?

2. What kind of severe climate changes have been happening?

2 Word Match

Match each word or phrase with its definition below.

(   ) **1. Glacier**s in Alaska have been shrinking dramatically since the 19th century.

(   ) **2.** Your actions online can have very serious **consequence**s for your future.

(   ) **3.** Plants **absorb** carbon dioxide from the air and give off oxygen.

(   ) **4.** Cyberattacks from other countries are **threaten**ing our national and economic security.

(   ) **5.** A large dam was built to prevent **flooding** in that area.

(   ) **6.** Australia has had several severe summer **drought**s in recent years.

(   ) **7.** The nuclear energy plan could cause **catastrophic** disasters to the environment.

(   ) **8.** The company was able to **adapt to** the COVID economy and improve its sales.

---

a. to take in something, such as a liquid or gas in a natural or gradual way

b. a result or effect of something

c. causing a lot of destruction, suffering, or death

d. a large amount of water covering an area that is usually dry

e. to cause damage or danger to something

f. to change your behavior in order to deal with a new situation more successfully

g. a large area of ice which moves very slowly, often down a mountain valley

h. a long period of time when there is little or no rain

---

3 Getting the Gist (First Viewing) [Time 02:20]

Watch the news and choose the right word in each statement.

1. Scientists spent the last three years looking at the (force / impact / weight) of climate change on glaciers and the seas.

2. This latest UN report found some of the more severe consequences of climate change can no longer be (avoided / examined / explained).

4 Getting into Details (Second Viewing) [Time 02:20]   1-38~40

Watch or listen to the news again. Fill in the blanks and answer the questions.

[1-38]

Tony Dokoupil: Moving on now to climate change. A highly anticipated UN climate change report out this morning raises the alarm about the ₁( ).

More than 100 scientists

5　spent the last three years looking at the impact of climate change on **glacier**s and the seas. Mark Phillips is in Monaco for us, where

10　the findings were released. Mark, what did we learn?

Mark Phillips: Good morning. Well, this report concerns the world's oceans and frozen regions. In other words, the North and South Poles and mountain tops. Its general conclusions – they can't ₂( ). The

15　**consequence**s for humanity, severe.

highly anticipated
大いに期待され（待たれ）ていた

raises the alarm
警鐘を鳴らしている

concerns ~
~に関係している

humanity
人類、人間

Comprehension Check

1. [T / F] The latest UN report gave us a wakeup call about the impact of climate change on the world's oceans and glaciers.
2. [T / F] The UN report studied all the world's oceans and frozen regions except for the North and South Poles.

[1-39]

Phillips: Until now, much of the Earth's warming has been **absorb**ed in its oceans. But according to this latest UN report, tipping points are

20　being reached … where some of the more severe consequences of climate change can ₃( ). Melting ice in Greenland and Antarctica and from mountain glaciers

warming
温度上昇

tipping points
〔重大な変化が起きる〕転換点

Antarctica
南極大陸

25 is continuing at accelerating rates. And the resulting

_4_(   ) around the world already

threatens coastal populations.

In the worst-case scenarios, as many as a billion people

could be affected. It may all sound like doomsday,

30 but one of the authors of the report, Arizona climate

scientist, Ted Schuur, says the signs of it _5_(

).

at accelerating rates
加速度的に

resulting ~
結果として生じる~

as many as ~
~もの数の

doomsday
世界滅亡の日

Comprehension Check

3. [T / F] The rate of melting ice in Greenland and Antarctica and from mountain
glaciers is increasing.

4. [T / F] People who are living near coastlines have not yet been affected by the
rising levels in seas and oceans.

5. [T / F] The reporter says the study results are so serious that it might sound like
the end of the world is coming.

[🎧1-40]

Ted Schuur: Looking at the time that those
events that happen one in 100

35 years _6_(

), and you can relate
to something like that where ...

Phillips: Major **flooding** event ... major inundation.

Schuur: Yeah, exactly. Imagine, imagine you have a story that

40 your grandfather told you about, you know, the town
flooding, but it was back 80 years ago. Well, _7_(
) every year.

Phillips: The report lists a cascade of potential negative effects, from
more severe storms to **drought**s to declining fish stocks.

45 And the more we continue to pump carbon dioxide
into the atmosphere, the more **catastrophic** those effects
may be. The report's authors say that we are now
_8_(   ) between the speed of climate

relate to ~
~を自分のことのように感じる

inundation
洪水、氾濫

back 80 years ago
80年も前の話

a cascade of ~
〔次々に起きる〕多くのもの［こと］

fish stocks
漁業資源

pump carbon dioxide into the atmosphere
二酸化炭素を大気に排出する

49

50 change and our ability to **adapt to** it, and that is the race that ₉(   ).

It's no longer a question of if or when the consequences will happen, but ₁₀(   ) they will be, Tony.

NEGATIVE EFFECTS ON OCEANS FROM CLIMATE CHANGE: **DROUGHTS**

55 **Dokoupil:** Frightening new details. Mark Phillips for us in Monaco. Mark, thank you very much.

Comprehension Check

6. [T / F] Dr. Schuur says that flooding events that usually happen once every 100 years now happen once a year.

7. [T / F] Dr. Schuur says his grandfather experienced a major flood 80 years ago.

8. [T / F] Severe storms, droughts, and declining fish stocks are some of the negative effects caused by climate change.

9. [T / F] The speed of climate change is moving faster than we can adapt to it.

5 Summary

🎵 **CD** 1-41

Fill in the blanks. The first two letters of each word are already given.

A new UN climate change report examined the impact of climate change on ₁(**gl**   ) and the seas. Much of the earth's warming has been ₂(**ab**   ) in its oceans. However, the report says the world's oceans can no longer handle the accelerating rates of ₃(**me**   ) ice in Greenland and Antarctica and from mountain glaciers. The ₄(**co**   ) of climate change are severe and have reached the tipping point. The sea level rise around the world already threatens coastal residents. ₅(**Fl**   ) events that usually happen once every 100 years now happen once a year. Severe storms, ₆(**dr**   ), and declining fish stocks are some of the negative effects of rising sea and ocean levels resulting from climate change. Increasing carbon dioxide in the atmosphere makes these effects even more ₇(**ca**   ). The speed of climate change is moving faster than we can ₈(**ad**   ) to it.

5

10

6 Conversation in Action

 1-42

Put the Japanese statements into English. Then listen to check your answers.

Emma: Hey, Jacob, why so *gloomy*?

Jacob: Well, I've been reading 1_____ for a class assignment. Here, have a look at the summary. （気候変動に関するこの国連の報告を）

Emma: Huh, it says we're already in a worst-case scenario because the 2_____

_____.

（地球温暖化の結果が転換点に達してしまった）

Jacob: Yeah. Until now the oceans have absorbed the Earth's warming. Glaciers are melting more quickly and there's more flooding, but there are more droughts, too.

Emma: And this situation is *threatening to* be even more catastrophic because

3_____.

（気候変動は我々がそれに適応できる以上に速く起きている）

Word Help *gloomy* 「暗い顔をしている」 *threaten to ~* 「～する恐れがある」

7 Critical Thinking

Discuss the following questions with your partner or group. Give reasons to support your opinions.

Understanding the News

1. What is the UN report in the news story about?
2. What are the results of the report?
3. Why are the scientists concerned?

What Would You Do?

1. Interview some older relatives and friends about climate change and their experiences when they were younger. Do they think environmental events are happening differently or more frequently now than in the past? Report your results to your group or class.
2. Do you think it's too late for us to prevent climate change? Why? / Why not?
3. Make a list of things you can do as an individual to slow or prevent climate change.

8 Cracking the Dress Code: #KuToo Movement

UNIT   Gender Equality / Activism

1 Before You Watch

Look at the title and photos and then answer the questions.

1. What is a dress code? Give some examples.

2. What does the term "movement" mean? What do you think is the aim of the #KuToo movement?

2 Word Match

Match each word with its definition below.

(   ) **1.** The research found that **discriminatory** practices were widespread in some companies.

(   ) **2.** The computer system at my university is hopelessly **outdated**.

(   ) **3.** Limiting the number of visitors to the World Heritage site has created a lot of **controversy**.

(   ) **4.** The corporate culture of many companies demands a certain **conformity** of appearance.

(   ) **5.** Many U.S. states have passed laws making it **mandatory** for rear seat passengers of motor vehicles to wear seatbelts.

(   ) **6.** Thousands of protesters gathered to support their **right**s to equality and freedom of expression.

(   ) **7.** The unpopular dress code was finally **abolish**ed about five years ago.

(   ) **8.** The price includes hotel and meals, but the short trip around the island is **optional**.

---

a. behavior that is the same as the behavior of most other people in a society, group, etc.

b. available as a choice but not required

c. something that you are morally, legally, or officially allowed to do or have

d. strong disagreement about something among a large group of people

e. to officially end or stop something, such as a system, practice, or institution

f. unfairly treating a person or group of people differently from other people or groups of people because of their religion, race, age, or gender

g. ordered by a law or rule

h. old and no longer suitable for modern purposes, methods, or situations

3 Getting the Gist (First Viewing) [Time 02:53]

Watch the news and choose the right word in each statement.

1. For Japanese working women, wearing high heels is considered good office (format / manners / society).

2. Followers of the #KuToo movement demand the right to wear (comfortable / easy / fashionable) footwear at work.

4 Getting into Details (Second Viewing) [Time 02:52] 2-02~04

Watch or listen to the news again. Fill in the blanks and answer the questions.

[2-02]

Dana Jacobson: Welcome back to CBS This Morning Saturday. We begin this half hour with the fashion backlash in Japan. There is an outcry on social media after a number of Japanese companies reportedly banned female employees ₁( ) to work.

5

Some women are calling the workplace rules **discriminatory** and **outdated**. And it doesn't end with eyeglasses. As Lucy Craft reports, the **controversy** is quite ₂( ) concerning female footwear in the workplace.

10

Lucy Craft: Activist Yumi Ishikawa has become the face of a ₃( ) in Japan. And her feet always shod in flat shoes are not just a fashion statement.

15

"Shoes are an expression of Japan's male chauvinism," she said. "It all comes down to ₄( )."

Taking a page from the

20

backlash	反発
outcry	激しい抗議
reportedly	報道によれば
concerning ~	~に関して
Activist	社会的変革を目指す活動家
~ shod in flat shoes	平らな靴を履いた~
male chauvinism	男性優越主義
Taking a page from ~	~を手本にして

#MeToo movement, Ishikawa and tens of thousands of followers have declared war on high heels. Their campaign is #KuToo, which means "shoe suffering."

declared war on ~
~に宣戦布告した

25

Comprehension Check

1. **[T / F]** Some women think the rules for what they can wear at work are discriminatory and outdated.
2. **[T / F]** Yumi Ishikawa started a social movement called #MeToo to protest Japan's male chauvinism.
3. **[T / F]** Ishikawa thinks a workplace rule that controls the kind of shoes women can wear is gender discrimination.
4. **[T / F]** #KuToo, which means "shoe suffering," is the name of a movement against company rules requiring women to wear high heels.

[🎧2-03]

Craft: Japan has been called the ₅(   ) for good reason. This nation's sartorial **conformity** starts early and continues throughout life.

sartorial
衣服に関する

30

High heels have become part of the dress code for working women in Japan. Wearing them is considered a kind of office etiquette. Even Japan's Labor Minister weighed in, calling ₆(   ) and reasonable.

weighed in
議論に加わった

35

Such was this entrenched male mindset in Japan that Ishikawa's old job at a funeral parlor where she spent six hours a day on her feet, heels were **mandatory**.

entrenched mindset
凝り固まった考え方
funeral parlor
葬儀場

"Three-inch heels were the rule," she said. "When quitting time rolled around, my toes were bleeding. I thought, 'Guys do the same job as me, why do they ₇(   ) flat shoes?'"

quitting time
退社時間

vented
（怒りなどの感情を）発散させた

40

Ishikawa vented online, and Japan felt her pain, literally. Scores of women shared horror stories about

Scores of ~
たくさんの~

45 grinning and bearing it through blisters, back pain, and hammertoes inflicted by prolonged high heel use. The #KuToo movement was

48.6K Tweets

石川優実@#KuToo署
@ishikawa_yumi

50 born, demanding the **right** to comfortable footwear at work.

blisters
（皮膚にできる）
まめ

hammertoes
槌状足指症

inflicted by ～
～で苦しめられた結
果引き起こされた

Comprehension Check

5. **[T / F]** Japan is known as the "land of uniforms" because rules for what can be worn start when people are young and continue as they grow older and become adults.

6. **[T / F]** Japan's Labor Minister says it is not necessary and rational for companies to have dress codes that require female staff to wear high heels.

7. **[T / F]** The #KuToo movement started when many Japanese women disagreed with Ishikawa's online complaints about wearing high heels.

[🎧2-04]

Craft: It's a movement that seems to have legs. Recently, major bank Sumitomo Mitsui **abolish**ed formal dress codes, a move $_8$( ).

have legs
うまく行く

55 "I think heels should be **optional**," said Kaname Kanamoto, an airline employee. "Requiring heels makes me wonder, 'Why aren't men wearing them?'"

"Traditional companies might require heels, but not newer, more progressive firms," said Saori Kikuchi,
60 who works in IT.

Meanwhile Ishikawa's turning her $_9$( ).
She's got a new book, and is about to debut her own line of sensible shoes. Another step toward $_{10}$(
).

debut her own line of sensible shoes
彼女自身が考えた一
連の履きやすい靴を
初めて売り出す

65 For CBS This Morning Saturday, Lucy Craft, Tokyo.

Comprehension Check

8. [T / F] A major Japanese bank opposed the #KuToo movement by refusing to put an end to their formal dress codes.

9. [T / F] Kaname Kanamoto thinks wearing high heels at work should not be mandatory.

10. [T / F] Ishikawa has not gained any benefits from her efforts to change Japanese workplace rules for wearing high heels.

♀ *Useful Tip*

#MeToo Movement — 被害を告発する「私も」運動とは

2017年10月、アメリカの大物ハリウッド映画プロデューサーによる女優たちへのセクハラ疑惑が報じられた際、彼女らが実名で告発したが、その後ある女優が同じような性的嫌がらせを受けた女性たちに向けて、"Me Too" と声を上げるように Twitter や Instagram などの SNS で呼びかけたことから始まったと言われている。それによって、多くの著名人や一般人が自身のセクハラ被害を告発し始め、現在もなお世界的なセクハラ告発の活動として広がっている。

5 Summary

🎵 2-05

Fill in the blanks. The first two letters of each word are already given.

There is an outcry on social media after several Japanese companies ₁(**ba**   ) female employees from wearing eyeglasses to work. Some women are calling the workplace rules ₂(**di**   ) and outdated. Another public controversy concerns female ₃(**fo**   ) in the workplace. Wearing high heels is part of the dress ₄(**co**   ) for working women, and wearing them is considered proper office etiquette. Activist Yumi Ishikawa has become the face of a new social ₅(**mo**   ). Ishikawa and thousands of followers have fought against wearing heels at work. Their campaign is #KuToo, which means "shoe ₆(**su**   )." They are demanding the ₇(**ri**   ) to wear comfortable footwear at work. Some women say wearing heels should be ₈(**op**   ) and not mandatory. It's difficult, because Japan's sartorial ₉(**co**   ) starts early and continues throughout life. However, the #KuToo movement is gaining support. Some companies have ₁₀(**ab**   ) rules for wearing heels. Ishikawa has also written a new book and has debuted her own line of workplace footwear for females.

5

10

15

6 **Conversation in Action**

 2-06

Put the Japanese statements into English. Then listen to check your answers.

Emma: Oww!

Jacob: Hey, Emma, what's wrong?

Emma: It's these shoes! My feet are *killing me*!

Jacob: Can't you wear more comfortable ones?

Emma: I want to, but I can't. Wearing high heels is a mandatory company dress code for women.

Jacob: What? That's unfair! There's no rule like that for men. It's so ₁_____ _____. (差別的で時代遅れな)

Emma: I know, I know. There's a new movement called #KuToo. Women are ₂_____ _____. I'm gonna join. (仕事場で快適な靴を履く権利を要求している)

Jacob: *Go for it!* Sometimes rules regarding conformity *die hard* in Japan. But I hope they abolish that rule soon.

Emma: Me too. Anyway, it all ₃_____. (結局は男女平等っていうところに行き着くわね)

Jacob: I agree. Well, it'll probably start a huge controversy, but it's worth it. Good luck!

Word Help   *killing me*: means a part of your body is hurting a lot. *Example:* My back is *killing me*.
Go for it!: means Do it! Try it! *Example:* I'm thinking of asking Katie out on a date. "Go for it".
die hard: means difficult to stop or to change slowly. *Example:* Old habits *die hard*, so it will take time to stop smoking.

---

7 **Conversation in Action**   **⚠ CHALLENGE**

Use the vocabulary and phrases you learned in Word Match and the news report scripts to make a short conversation with your partner. Then practice your conversation with your partner or group.

_____: _____
(Name)

_____: _____
(Name)

_____: _____
(Name)

_____: _____
(Name)

8 Critical Thinking

Discuss the following questions with your partner or group. Give reasons to support your opinions.

Understanding the News

1. Why are some women calling workplace rules discriminatory and outdated?

2. What does the sentence, "Shoes are an expression of Japan's male chauvinism" mean?

3. What is the #KuToo movement? How did it start?

What Would You Do?

1. Do you think women should be required to wear high heels at work? What do you think are some other examples of gender inequality in Japan?

2. What is your opinion of dress codes? Give some examples of dress codes for social events, school, or business in Japan or in your country. What would happen if you did not follow the rules?

3. Can you think of any rules in Japanese society that are discriminatory or outdated? Give some examples and include your opinion on whether or how they might change or not.

9 Grammar Table Lady Offers Advice

UNIT

Language / Human Interest

1 Before You Watch

Look at the title and photos and then answer the questions.

1. What do you think the woman sitting at the table is doing in the photos above?

2. Do you think most people have difficulty using correct grammar?

2 Word Match

Match each word or phrase with its definition below.

(   ) **1.** She spoke with **passion** about preserving the environment.

(   ) **2.** A knowledge of **linguistics** is useful when you want to study and analyze the structure of different languages.

(   ) **3.** He's been struggling to beat his **addiction** to online gaming.

(   ) **4.** I need some more storage space on my smartphone, but I don't want to **leave out** any of my pictures from the photos app.

(   ) **5.** A neutral third party was brought in to settle the **dispute**.

(   ) **6.** We hope that the conflict can be **resolve**d peacefully.

(   ) **7.** Steve Jobs' 2005 Stanford commencement speech is very exciting and **enlightening**. You should watch it on YouTube.

(   ) **8.** I know I should eat less, but I **can't help but** have some dessert.

---

a. a disagreement or argument

b. the scientific study of language or of particular languages

c. cannot stop yourself from doing something

d. giving you more information and a better understanding of something

e. a strong and harmful desire to regularly have something or do something

f. a very strong feeling of love or excitement for something or about doing something

g. to find an answer or solution to solve something

h. to not include someone or something

---

3 Getting the Gist (First Viewing) [Time 03:03]

Watch the news and choose the right word in each statement.

1. The reporter (confused / explained / used) grammar related words to make the news report interesting and amusing.

2. Ellen Jovin set up a table on New York City streets and (started / studied / suggested) giving grammar advice because she has a passion for grammar.

4 **Getting into Details (Second Viewing)** [Time 03:03] DVD 2-08~10

Watch or listen to the news again. Fill in the blanks and answer the questions.

[🎵2-08]

Margaret Brennan: In an imperfect world, Steve Hartman found someone with a **passion** for the ₁( ). You can put an exclamation point on that. Here's tonight's On The Road.

5 **Steve Hartman:** Imagine you're out walking, shopping, or doing some other gerund ...

Ellen Jovin: Hello.

Hartman: ... when out of nowhere ...

10 **Jovin:** Give me a ₂( )!

Hartman: ... a woman on the street prepositions you.

Jovin: "Over" is a preposition. "Under" is a preposition.

Hartman: What would you think?

Jovin: People must ₃( ) when you know
15 this kind of stuff.

Hartman: You might think, whom is this crazy lady ...

Jovin: Do you have any grammar questions?

Hartman: ... who sees grammar as such
an imperative that she sets
20 up a table just to ₄(
).

Jovin: 'Cause I love grammar so much
and also ...

Hartman: You couldn't think of anything more interesting?

exclamation point
感嘆符

gerund
動名詞

when out of nowhere
その時どこからともなく

prepositions
本来はpropositions
「誘いをかける」となるべき
preposition
前置詞

whom is ~
文法的にはwhoが正しいが、ここではわざと間違えている

imperative
重要・必須であること（文法用語では「命令形」の意）

25 *Jovin:* But it's the anchor. Like right now, we're using words. This wouldn't even be happening. We'd just be looking at each other.

Comprehension Check

1. **[T / F]** Ellen Jovin thinks that people are impressed by good grammar.
2. **[T / F]** The main reason Jovin likes to give advice about grammar is because she thinks people make too many grammar mistakes.
3. **[T / F]** Jovin thinks good grammar makes it possible for us to communicate by using words and the structure of language correctly.

[💿 2-09]

Hartman: By day, Ellen Jovin runs a company training people in

30 business communications. But her real passion is **linguistics**. She has a huge library of grammar and stylebooks from Arabic to Zulu ... to ₅(

) and have

35 some fun. Last year she began setting up her grammar table around New York City, where she lives. And it went so well she is now taking the table to the collective noun that is America.

stylebook
句読点や記号、文体などについての表記法をまとめた本

Zulu
（南アフリカの）ズールー語

collective noun
集合名詞

Jovin: You know, on the road around the country ...

40 *Hartman:* We caught up with her here in New Hope, Pennsylvania, where Ellen spent the day ₆(   ) how to diagram sentences ...

Jovin: I bet you remember this.

Hartman: ... explaining when to use "who" and "whom" ...

diagram sentences
文の構造がわかるように略図を書く

I bet ~
きっと~よ

45 *Jovin:* "Whom," and do you know why?

Hartman: ... and counseling people on their comma **addiction**s.

Jovin: Are you a comma user?

Man: Yes, I am. I probably overuse them.

50 *Jovin:* We ... we have a little bit more of an urge to **leave** them **out** sometimes.

a little bit more of an urge to ~
〜したいというちょっとした衝動のようなもの

Comprehension Check

4. [T / F] Giving grammar advice to passersby on the street is Jovin's main job.

5. [T / F] Jovin's passion is sharing her love of linguistics with others.

6. [T / F] Jovin began setting up her grammar advice table in libraries around New York City last year.

7. [T / F] Jovin's grammar advice table was very successful in New York City, so she decided to take it to other cities across America.

8. [T / F] Jovin thinks people have a tendency to not use commas when they should.

[🎧 2-10]

Hartman: She even answered something I've always wondered about. Does the period $_7($ $)$ the quotation mark, or can it go outside in certain circumstances?

55 How about *The story Steve did on the grammar lady was "interesting."*? Where does the period go there? Because I'm using "interesting" in like, an
60 ironic way.

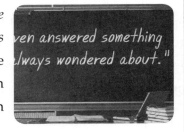

Jovin: Yes, I understand that completely. But it always goes inside.

Jovin: So in this sentence ...

Hartman: But Ellen says $_8($ $)$ is settling grammar **dispute**s between husbands and wives.

65 *Jovin:* I **resolve** that. And I feel good about that.

Hartman: She says it's been very ... **enlightening**.

Jovin: In my experience, usually if a couple comes up, usually the

70 woman is right. I mean, in … in my limited experience.

Hartman: I'm … I'm grammarless right now.

She hung me out like a dangling modifier. But you **can't help but** love her passion. And a lot of people do appreciate her mission. This guy at a red light just had to know, right then and there, "Do you always capitalize after a colon?"

75

Jovin: If it's only a piece of a sentence, definitely no cap.

80 **Man in the car:** OK.

Jovin: Yeah.

Hartman: That ₉(   ).

Jovin: Bye.

Hartman: One more convert, in Ellen's ever-growing army of grammar defenders.

85

Jovin: You will be intensely popular because people love to be corrected on their grammar.

Hartman: Next lesson … sarcasm.

90 *Jovin:* Thank you for stopping by!

Hartman: Steve Hartman, On The Road, in New Hope, Pennsylvania.

grammarless
本来はspeechless
となるべきところ

hung me out
私をつるして
ブラブラさせた
（danglingからき
た表現）

**dangling
modifier**
懸垂修飾語
⇒章末Useful Tip
参照

appreciate
〜を高く評価する

definitely no cap
絶対に大文字にし
ない

convert
改宗者

**ever-growing
army of
grammar
defenders**
ますます増大する文
法を擁護する軍団

sarcasm
皮肉

Comprehension Check

9. **[T / F]** Jovin tells the reporter that a period doesn't always go inside a quotation mark.
10. **[T / F]** She enjoys resolving disagreements between husbands and wives about using correct grammar.
11. **[T / F]** The reporter thinks Jovin is being sarcastic when she says people enjoy having their grammar mistakes corrected.

5 Summary 2-11

Fill in the blanks. The first two letters of each word are already given.

Ellen Jovin runs a company training people in business communications. But her real ₁(**pa**   ) is linguistics. She says that people can't ₂(**he**   ) but be impressed by someone who knows how to use good grammar. Last year, she began setting up a ₃(**gr**   ) table on the streets of New York City to ₄(**sh**   ) her knowledge and have some fun. Her ₅(**mi**   ) is to answer questions people have about using correct grammar. She explains how to diagram sentences and use commas because people sometimes ₆(**le**   ) them out. She also gives advice on how to capitalize words and when to use "who" or "whom." Ellen says her experience is ₇(**en**   ) and she enjoys resolving grammar ₈(**di**   ) between husbands and wives. She says that when a couple has a disagreement about grammar, the woman is usually right. Her grammar table was so popular in New York City that she decided to try it in other cities.

5

10

♀ Useful Tip

dangling modifier（懸垂修飾語）とは

次の英文を見てください。どこか変ですね。

Looking around the yard, dandelions sprouted in every corner.

タンポポ (dandelions) がこの文の主語ですが、Looking の主語は誰でしょうか。通常英語の場合、分詞は主文の主語と一致しなければなりません。このままでは Looking の主語が dandelions となり、タンポポが庭を見渡していることになります。本当は庭を見渡しているのは人間の私です。この文を読む人は意味はなんとなくつかめるけれども、すわりの悪い変な感じを受けるのです。文法的に正しい文にするにはコンマの前後でそれぞれの主語を一致させる必要があります。

Looking around the yard, I could see that dandelions sprouted in every corner.

上記のようにすると「庭を見渡す主体」と「タンポポを見ている主体」が同一となり、すわりのよい文となるのです。英語話者でも多くの人が犯す誤りの一つです。

本文ではレポーターの Hartman が She hung me out like a dangling modifier. と言っていますが、「懸垂修飾語を使うことで人を惑わしてしまう文のように、彼女は私をつるしブラブラした (dangling) 状態にして私を当惑させた」、つまり、「私は当惑してしまった」という意味になります。

6 Conversation in Action

 2-12

Put the Japanese statements into English. Then listen to check your answers.

Emma: Jacob, can you help me with this cover letter for my resume?

Jacob: Sure, Emma. Hmm. I'm impressed. I can see you ₁_____

_____. (法律と人々を助けることについて情熱を持っている)

Emma: Yeah. ₂_____

between big city governments and local communities. (私の使命は不和を解決するのに役に立つことなの)

Jacob: That would definitely be an enlightening experience. But I couldn't help but notice that ₃_____.

You forgot to capitalize some words, too. (君がコンマをいくつか省いてしまっている)

Emma: Oh, really? *Good eye*, Jacob! Thanks a lot.

> **Word Help**   ***Good eye***: slang for a special ability to notice or recognize a particular thing or quality. *Example:* He has a *good eye* for details.

7 Critical Thinking

Discuss the following questions with your partner or group. Give reasons to support your opinions.

Understanding the News

1. What is Ellen Jovin passionate about?

2. What did Ellen do to share her passion with others? Why?

3. The reporter uses word play (the clever and witty use of words and their meaning) to make his news report more interesting and amusing. Give some examples.

What Would You Do?

1. Do you know the grammar terms the reporter uses? Write the definition and give an example of each term. Include other terms you think are useful to know and remember.

2. The reporter asks Ellen about a grammar point that is difficult for him. ("Does the period have to go inside the quotation mark, or can it go outside in certain circumstances?") Give an example of a grammar point that is difficult for you when learning English.

3. Ellen has a passion for linguistics. What is your passion? Why? How do you enjoy and share it with others?

10 Halloween Treats for Kids with Disabilities

Holiday / Volunteerism

1 Before You Watch

Look at the title and photos and then answer the questions.

1. What is Halloween, and what is a Halloween treat?

2. What kinds of difficulties do you think kids with disabilities might have when celebrating Halloween?

2 Word Match

Match each word or phrase with its definition below.

(　) **1.** Studying in the English Track Program at my university is **challenging**, but my language skills have improved a lot.

(　) **2.** We need a more creative **solution** to this problem.

(　) **3.** Some parents think having **sibling**s makes kids happier, but research data shows it doesn't matter.

(　) **4.** What should I do to **sign up** for the online banking service?

(　) **5.** You have to **submit** your assignment by the end of this week.

(　) **6.** The area was **transform**ed from a quiet farming village into a busy city.

(　) **7.** Tim gives a large **donation** to his favorite charity every year.

(　) **8.** The accident was a timely **reminder** of just how dangerous texting while driving can be.

---

a. to register someone's name on an official list in order to get, do, or take something

b. a way of solving a problem or dealing with a difficult situation

c. something that makes you remember something else

d. to hand in or send something (report, application, etc.) to someone so that they can consider it or decide about it

e. to completely change the appearance or character of something/somebody

f. something (such as money, food, clothes, etc.) that is given to help a person or organization

g. difficult in a way that tests your ability and is hard to achieve

h. a brother or sister

---

3 Getting the Gist (First Viewing) [Time 03:52]

Watch the news and choose the right word in each statement.

1. The Halloween tradition of trick-or-treating can be (difficult / forgotten / unfamiliar) for kids with physical disabilities.

2. Hospital staff and volunteers at the Shriners Hospitals (create / display / sell) Halloween costumes for children who use wheelchairs.

4 Getting into Details (Second Viewing) [Time 03:52]   2-14~17

Watch or listen to the news again. Fill in the blanks and answer the questions.

[2-14]

Anthony Mason: In our series, A More Perfect Union, we aim to show that what unites us as Americans is far greater than what divides us. Today is Halloween, of course, and for kids that means ₁( ).

But door-to-door trick-or-treating can be **challenging** for kids with physical disabilities. We visited one Utah hospital that found a creative **solution** to make sure all kids get a treat this Halloween.

Cole Spencer: I really wish I could have superpowers. If there's trouble, then I could save the world.

Jamie Yuccas: It's a big dream for a little kid ... who's already ₂( ). Cole Spencer was diagnosed with spina bifida, a birth defect of the spine, when his mom was five months pregnant.

Cole's mom: OK. This one's for the win! Whoo!

Yuccas: Now, five years old, he has no problem keeping up with his older **sibling**s, except when it comes to trick-or-treating.

Cole's mom: Trick or treat!

Yuccas: It was hard for him to reach the door to collect candy.

Woman: Probably can't get much closer …

Cole's mom: Halloween's a hard thing when you are in a wheelchair

far
はるかに（比較級を強める）

treat
特別な楽しみ

was diagnosed with spina bifida
脊椎披裂と診断された
birth defect of the spine 先天性脊椎障害
This one's for the win! これが決勝点よ！

or if you are in any state of $_3$(   ).

Comprehension Check

1. **[T / F]** The reporter says the aim of the "A More Perfect Union" series is to show positive stories that help bring Americans together.
2. **[T / F]** Cole Spencer can play and do many other activities with his siblings except when trick-or-treating at Halloween.
3. **[T / F]** When Cole goes trick-or-treating, he can reach the door to collect Halloween candy by himself.

[🎧 2-15]

Yuccas: Four-year-old Cooper Baskett, who was born with a form
30   of dwarfism, faced similar challenges.

	a form of dwarfism 小人症の一種

Cooper's Mom: Trick-or-treating was just rough because he wouldn't get candy. His brother would bring it back for him.
35   And he slowly, quickly lost interest.

rough つらい、苦しい

Yuccas: When Baskett and Spencer heard about the wheelchair costume clinic at Shriners Hospitals for Children, they **sign**ed **up** immediately. The kids **submit** their ideas.
40   And hospital staff and volunteers $_4$(   ). But it's when the kids arrive that the volunteers work their magic.

Shriners Hospitals for Children 米ソルトレークシティにある子ども病院

work their magic 魔法（のような力）を使った

Comprehension Check

4. **[T / F]** Although Cooper has a different disability, he has the same difficulty when trick-or-treating as Cole.
5. **[T / F]** Cooper wouldn't get candy when he went trick-or-treating because he didn't have a costume.
6. **[T / F]** The staff at the Shriners Hospitals wheelchair costume clinic submit their ideas for costumes and the children design them.

[🎧 2-16]

Yuccas: With the help of cardboard, PVC pipe, some paint and glue, kids in their wheelchairs are **transform**ed into

cardboard 段ボール

PVC polyvinyl chloride ポリ塩化ビニル

45　　　everything from a DJ spinning records, and Disney's
　　　　Moana and her canoe … to Superman in his phone
　　　　booth and Rapunzel in her tower.

Yuccas: Scott Jerome works for Shriners. He says the program
　　　　helped 32 kids this year – the largest group since it
50　　　started four years ago.

Scott Jerome: It's fun to see them be a child …
　　　　and enjoy what they're doing.

Yuccas: The costumes cost up to $150 to
　　　　build, but the program is
55　　　supported by **donation** and
　　　　dozens of ₅(　　　　　　　　　).

up to ~
最高〜まで

Yuccas: Jerome says the flashy creations …

flashy creations
派手な創作物

Little girl in costume: I'm in … a princess dress.

Yuccas: … encouraged candy givers to leave their doorsteps, just
60　　　the trick to help these kids get their treats.

trick
うまいやり方、効果
的な方法

Comprehension Check

7. [T / F] The wheelchair costume program at Shriners Hospitals for Children was established 32 years ago.

8. [T / F] The parents of children who participate in the wheelchair costume program pay for the costume materials.

9. [T / F] The creative wheelchair costumes encourage people to move closer to the children when they hand out candy.

[🎧2-17]

Jerome: I think what brings us back as well is the stories that we
　　　　get from the families … that Halloween starts to come
　　　　to them.

what brings us back as well
私たちが毎年ここに
戻って来てこのよう
な事を行うのは

Little girl: They did a good job on it. At
65　　　my school, it's gonna be
　　　　crazy. Everyone's gonna
　　　　look at me.

Yuccas: Cole is ready to save the world.

Cole: Batman!

70 *Cole's mom:* I think all parents with kids with disabilities just really want their kids to have the experience of $_6$(

)

75 would have ... and when you get a glimpse of it, it just warms your heart.

Yuccas: And Cooper is Forky, a popular *Toy Story 4* character in his RV.

Cooper: Thank you!

80 *Cooper's mom:* Just to see his little face light up and spark up and $_7$(   ). When they roll away in their costumes, you've made a

85 dream come true for them.

Yuccas: It's a timely **reminder** that costumes not only allow kids to become someone else, they can help show the world $_8$(   ).

Jerome: It's just Batman!

90 *Yuccas:* For CBS This Morning, Jamie Yuccas, Salt Lake City.

get a glimpse of ~
～を一目見る

RV
recreational vehicle（キャンピングカー）

roll away
車に乗って走り去る

Comprehension Check

10. [T / F] The Shriners Hospitals for Children staff and volunteers enjoy hearing from parents about their children's experiences.

11. [T / F] Cole's mom says the wheelchair costume program enables children with disabilities to have the same kind of experience that a normal child would have at Halloween.

12. [T / F] The reporter says that wearing a costume is not so special because it only allows kids to pretend to be someone else.

5 Summary

2-18

Fill in the blanks. The first two letters of each word are already given.

For kids, Halloween means costumes and candy. But door-to-door trick-or-treating can be ₁(**ch**   ) for children with physical disabilities. Although Cole Spencer and Cooper Baskett have no trouble keeping up with their ₂(**si**   ), they both have difficulty with trick-or-treating. Neither Cole nor Cooper can reach the door to collect candy. Shriners   5
Hospitals for Children in Utah found a creative ₃(**so**   ) to make sure that all kids get a treat at Halloween. Parents ₄(**si**   ) up their kids at the hospital's wheelchair costume clinic. Then the kids submit their ideas and hospital staff and volunteers ₅(**de**   ) the costumes. The cost of building the costumes is supported by donation. The   10
creative wheelchair costumes ₆(**en**   ) people to move closer to the children when they hand out candy. The parents of kids with disabilities are happy that their kids can experience Halloween like a normal child. It's a dream come true for the children, and a timely ₇(**re**   ) that costumes can help show the world ₈(**wh**   ) they really are.   15

6 Conversation in Action

2-19

Put the Japanese statements into English. Then listen to check your answers.

Emma: Hey, cool Superman costume, Jacob!

Jacob: Ha ha, thanks. I'm volunteering to ₁_____
_____. (障がいを持つ子どもたちのためにハロウィーン用の衣装を作る)

Emma: Oh, I've heard about that. The local hospital has a wheelchair costume clinic, right?

Jacob: Yeah. Kids ₂_____.
(申し込みをして自分たちの案を送るんだよ、そして、僕らがその衣装を作るんだ)

Emma: Sounds great! How can I help?

Jacob: Well, you can ₃_____ build costumes.
(寄付をするか来て僕らを手伝って)

Emma: *I'm in.* Wow, you really are a superhero!

Word Help   * *I'm in.* : another way of saying "Count me in," which means "Include me."
Example: That's a good plan. I'm in.

7 Conversation in Action ⚠ CHALLENGE

Use the vocabulary and phrases you learned in Word Match and the news report scripts to make a short conversation with your partner. Then practice your conversation with your partner or group.

_____: _____
(Name)

_____: _____
(Name)

_____: _____
(Name)

_____: _____
(Name)

8 Critical Thinking

Discuss the following questions with your partner or group. Give reasons to support your opinions.

Understanding the News

1. Why can door-to-door trick-or-treating be challenging for kids with physical disabilities?

2. What creative solution did Shriners Hospitals for Children find to assure that kids with disabilities get a treat at Halloween?

3. How did this creative solution help physically disabled children get treats when they go trick-or-treating?

What Would You Do?

1. Why do people wear costumes at Halloween?

2. Have you ever worn a Halloween costume, or gone trick-or-treating, or attended a Halloween Party? Describe or show a picture of a costume you wore to your partner or group.

3. Is Halloween celebrated in your country? How?

11 A Tax on Tourism?

A TAX ON TOURISM?
VENICE CHARGING FOR ACCESS TO ITALIAN CITY

1 Before You Watch

Look at the title and photos and then answer the questions.

1. Do you think Venice is popular with tourists? Why?

2. Why do you think the city of Venice wants to tax tourists?

2 Word Match

Match each word or phrase with its definition below.

( ) **1.** A new UN climate report warns civilization could be **at stake** if we don't act now.

( ) **2.** That area of the city was **infamous** for poverty and crime many years ago.

( ) **3.** The new **measure** regarding the tax reduction was approved by Parliament.

( ) **4.** The latest incident has **strain**ed relations between the two countries.

( ) **5.** Jenny was fascinated by the traditional **architecture** found in places like Nara and Kyoto.

( ) **6.** This small music box is extremely **fragile**, so please handle it with care.

( ) **7.** I got a $100 **fine** for speeding.

( ) **8.** We will be **implement**ing a new scheme to improve our sales next year.

---

a. the design or style of a building or buildings

b. something that is at risk and might be lost or damaged if not successful

c. weak and easily broken or damaged

d. to begin to do or use something, such as a plan; to make something active or effective

e. a sum of money that must be paid as punishment for breaking a law or rule

f. an official plan introduced by the government to deal with a problem

g. to injure or weaken by force, stress, pressure, etc.

h. well known for some bad quality or action

---

3 Getting the Gist (First Viewing) [Time 02:52]

Watch the news and choose the right word in each statement.

1. To stop overcrowding, Venice wants tourists who don't stay overnight in hotels to pay an entrance (amount / charge / price).

2. The huge number of daily visitors is not only putting stress on the city's resources and delicate architecture, but also causing Venice to lose its (emotion / energy / identity).

4 Getting into Details (Second Viewing) [Time 02:52] DVD 2-21~23

Watch or listen to the news again. Fill in the blanks and answer the questions.

[2-21]

Norah O'Donnell: A controversial new proposal aims to stop
₁(   ) in one
of the world's most popular
tourist destinations.

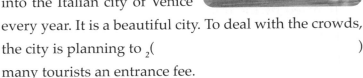

5 About 30 million visitors pack
into the Italian city of Venice
every year. It is a beautiful city. To deal with the crowds,
the city is planning to ₂(   )
many tourists an entrance fee.

10 Seth Doane is in Venice, where locals say the city's future
is **at stake**. Seth, good morning.

Seth Doane: Good morning to you.
Locals say this place has
₃(   )
15 it is like a Disneyland for
tourists. This view has always
been seen as priceless, but
now it in fact may come with a price, upwards of 10
euros, that's the U.S. equivalent of about 11 dollars and
20 50 cents for a visit.

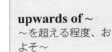

tourist destinations
観光地、旅行先

pack into ~
（集団で）〜に押しかける

upwards of ~
〜を超える程度、およそ〜

the U.S. equivalent of ~
米国では〜に相当する額

Comprehension Check

1. [T / F] The purpose of the new proposal is to stop overcrowding in Venice by charging tourists an entrance fee to visit.
2. [T / F] Local residents are not very worried about the future of Venice.
3. [T / F] Local residents say tourists prefer to visit Disneyland more than Venice.

[2-22]

Doane: Its famed canals and picture-perfect setting has [sic] made
Venice **infamous** for its tourists. Hordes pack its narrow
alleys searching for that all-important selfie, but the vast

Hordes pack its narrow alleys
群衆が狭い路地に詰めかける

25 majority – about ₄(   )
of visitors – do not spend the night. So the city loses out
on potential earnings from hotel taxes.

Now, Italy's Parliament has approved a **measure** that'll
allow the city to charge tourists that only come for the
day.

30 *Mayor Luigi Brugnaro / Doane (voice-over translation):* The money would
go towards keeping the city
clean, Mayor Luigi Brugnaro
said, and allow locals to
live with more decorum.
35 Venetians have told us they're
concerned the daily deluge of
visitors, some coming on giant cruise ships, is not only
straining the city's resources and delicate **architecture,**
but causing Venice ₅(   ).

40 *Doane:* Since 1951, the city's population has plummeted to fewer
than 55,000 people, but it can see, on average, more than
80,000 visitors per day.

We reported on the regular protests from residents who
carried suitcases as a symbol they're on their way out.

lose out on ~
〜を逃す

go towards ~
（金が）〜に使わ
れる

decorum
気品、尊厳

deluge of ~
おびただしい数の

plummeted to ~
〜に激減した

Comprehension Check

4. [T / F] Most tourists do not stay overnight in Venice, so the city cannot receive money from hotel taxes.

5. [T / F] The new tax will require tourists who stay overnight in Venice to pay an entrance fee.

6. [T / F] The money collected from the entrance fee will be used to help clean the city and make Venice a more dignified and respectful place to live.

7. [T / F] The population of Venice has been increasing since 1951.

8. [T / F] Protesters carry suitcases as a symbol to persuade more people to come and live in Venice.

[🎧2-23]

45 *Paola Mar:* We have many, many ... too much tourists.

Doane: Too many tourists.

Mar: Yes.

Doane: That's according to Paola Mar, who manages tourism for the city. Before the new tax was announced, she told us visitors are $_6$( ), but the city has reached a breaking point.

breaking point
（忍耐などの）
限界点

Doane (voice-over translation): Tourists are our guests, Mar told us. And we want to treat them with respect. But we want respect. This is a **fragile** city.

Doane: Officials have put up gates so they can control the flow and have proposed raising a **fine** to more than 500 dollars for those sitting or lying on undesignated public spaces. They've also banned the opening of new $_7$( ) out of concern Venice was at risk of losing its identity.

put up gates
出入り口を設置した

undesignated
指定外の

out of concern ～
～という心配から

The tax will be higher during peak periods, though it is not yet clear when or how this fee will be **implement**ed, though it is certain that other cities facing this tourist crush $_8$( ) Venice closely.

tourist crush
観光客による大混雑

Comprehension Check

9. [T / F] Paola Mar says tourists are important to the economy, but that the city is too fragile and cannot put up with any more overcrowding.

10. [T / F] City officials have set up gates to control the movement of tourists, and have also increased the penalty for people using public spaces where sitting or lying down are not allowed.

11. [T / F] Venetian city officials have encouraged the opening of new fast-food chains so tourists will have more places to eat.

12. [T / F] The reporter says that the new entrance fee will start in the peak season.

13. [T / F] Other cities that have problems with too many tourists are watching to see what will happen when Venice implements the new entrance fee.

5 Summary

CD 2-24

Fill in the blanks. The first two letters of each word are already given.

The Italian city of Venice is one of the most popular travel destinations in the world and is ₁(**in**   ) for its tourists. But Venice's popularity is causing problems for its residents. Locals worry that Venice's future is at ₂(**st**   ) because it is too ₃(**fr**   ). Most tourists do not stay overnight in Venice, so the city cannot receive money from hotel taxes. City officials are concerned the huge number of daily visitors is not only ₄(**st**   ) the city's resources and delicate architecture, but also causing Venice to lose its ₅(**id**   ). To deal with the crowds, Parliament approved a controversial new ₆(**me**   ) to start charging many tourists an ₇(**en**   ) fee, and city officials increased fines. New fast food restaurants will be banned. The new tax and fines will help improve decorum and keep the city clean. Other cities facing the same tourist problems are watching to see what will happen when Venice ₈(**im**   ) the new entrance fee.

5

10

6 Conversation in Action

CD 2-25

Put the Japanese statements into English. Then listen to check your answers.

Emma: I just got an email from my host mom in Venice.

Jacob: What did she say? I've heard it's ₁_____.

                           （多くの観光客でひどく評判が悪い）

Emma: Umm … not since the pandemic. Like everywhere else, the coronavirus has had a huge effect on tourism.

Jacob: I guess even before that happened, they were concerned about the huge strain on city resources, and how fragile Venice really is.

Emma: Uh huh. Some controversial measures and fines were about to be ₂_____ _____.

         （過剰な人々の集まりを制御するために実施される）

Jacob: She must be very worried. ₃_____.

              （ベニスの未来は危機に瀕することになるだろう）

Emma: Yeah, everyone is thinking about ways to *reopen the city. And how to improve

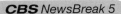

the *quality of life* for Venetians and visitors.

Jacob: I hope everything gets better soon.

> **Word Help**   *reopen:* to begin to operate a place or business or to become available for people to
> use after being closed for a period of time
> *quality of life:* the degree to which a person or group is healthy, comfortable, and
> able to enjoy the activities of daily living

7   Critical Thinking

Discuss the following questions with your partner or group. Give reasons to support your opinions.

Understanding the News

1. Why are the residents of Venice concerned about their city's future?

2. What effect is this problem having on Venice?

3. How is Venice planning to deal with this problem?

What Would You Do?

1. Do you think tourism is important? Why?/Why not? Discuss some advantages and disadvantages with your partner or group.

2. Which country in the world do you think is the most popular tourist destination? What is its capital? What are the top three tourist attractions?

3. What do you think is the most popular tourist attraction in Japan for visitors from foreign countries? Why? Describe it.

Japan Really Loves Kit Kat Bars

1 Before You Watch

Look at the title and photos and then answer the questions.

1. Have you ever had a Kit Kat bar? If yes, how did it taste? If not, why haven't you tried it yet?

2. Why do you think Kit Kat bars are so popular in Japan?

2 Word Match

Match each word or phrase with its definition below.

(   ) **1.** Ted has an **obsession** with Pokémon video games. He has all the latest apps and accessories.

(   ) **2.** This expensive T-shirt design is a collaboration between a famous **luxury** brand and a street artist.

(   ) **3.** She turned out to be the **mastermind** behind the secret project.

(   ) **4.** Traditional Japanese **confection**s, called *wagashi*, have a delicate sweetness that dissolves in the mouth.

(   ) **5.** Some people prefer a more **aggressive** taste when it comes to eating curry.

(   ) **6.** *Omamori* is a Japanese **talisman** that many people believe brings good fortune and protection.

(   ) **7.** Many Japanese companies **capitalize on** *kawaii* (cute) logo characters for their businesses.

(   ) **8.** I'm graduating next year. I wonder how I should **go about** job-hunting?

> **a.** an intelligent person who plans and directs a complicated project or activity
> **b.** to use a situation to help you achieve something or get an advantage from something
> **c.** to begin an activity or start working on solving a problem
> **d.** a thing that is expensive and pleasant, but not essential
> **e.** an object that is believed to have magic powers and to bring good luck
> **f.** very strong or intense
> **g.** a sweet food that looks very attractive
> **h.** something that a person thinks about constantly or frequently in a way that is not normal

3 Getting the Gist (First Viewing) [Time 03:46]

Watch the news and choose the right word in each statement.

1. The Japanese pronunciation of "Kit Kat" is (common / equal / similar) to *kitto katsu*, which in Japanese, means, "You surely will win!"

2. Visitors to Japan are (attracted / encouraged / persuaded) to Japanese Kit Kat flavors because they read on social media that they are fantastic and want to try them.

4 **Getting into Details (Second Viewing)** [Time 03:46]   2-27~30

Watch or listen to the news again. Fill in the blanks and answer the questions.

[2-27]

Anchor: *Kitto Katto* is more than the Japanese name for the candy we all know as Kit Kat. It's Japan's national **obsession**. Here's Mo Rocca.

Mo Rocca: At a shop in Tokyo's bustling Ginza district, **luxury** Kit
5   Kats ₁(   ). That's right: luxury Kit Kats! And the **mastermind** behind these five-dollar Kit Kat **confection**s is pastry chef Yasumasa Takagi.

Rocca: "In general," says chef Takagi, "the Japanese ₂(
10   ) rather than **aggressive** flavors that hit you over the head."

    Takagi's   concocted   Kit
    Kats   with   flavors   like
    matcha   green   tea,   butter,
15   and   strawberry   maple.

bustling
にぎやかな

pastry chef
菓子職人・パティ
シエ

**that hit you over
the head**
頭にガツンと来る
ような
concocted
混ぜて作った

Comprehension Check

1. **[T / F]** The news reporter says premium Kit Kats sold in Tokyo's Ginza district are more luxurious and more expensive than those in America.
2. **[T / F]** Yasumasa Takagi is the chef who creates the flavors for luxury Kit Kats at the Ginza district store.
3. **[T / F]** Takagi says Japanese like strong flavors more than mild ones.

[2-28]

Rocca: Cedric Lacroix is Kit Kat's man in Japan.

    How big is the Kit Kat in Japan?

Cedric Lacroix: Kit Kat is very, very big.
    We consume ₃(
20   ) Kit
    Kats a day in Japan.

Rocca: (Whistles) … You might call its popularity a case of Kit Kat kismet.

kismet
運命、宿命

Rocca: *Kitto Katto*, the Japanese pronunciation of Kit Kat, sounds an awful lot like *kitto katsu*, which in Japanese means 'You surely will win!'

"You surely will win!"

an awful lot
とても

Which ₄(   ), for Japanese students during the high-pressure exam season, the *kitto katto* has become a kind of edible **talisman**.

Rocca: When it was discovered that the name meant 'surely you will win,' …

Lacroix: Yes …

Rocca: … then the company shrewdly decided to **capitalize on** that.

shrewdly
抜け目なく、ちゃっかり

Lacroix: Absolutely, absolutely. And it became part of the ₅(   ) to … to … to play this lucky charm. So Kit Kat's mission in Japan is … is really to … to encourage people.

play ~
～をうまく使う

Comprehension Check

4. **[T / F]** Cedric Lacroix is the manager of the Kit Kat company in Japan.
5. **[T / F]** The Japanese pronunciation of Kit Kat - *Kitto Katto* - sounds like a Japanese phrase that means 'lucky charm.'
6. **[T / F]** The Kit Kat company used the similarity between *Kitto Katto* and *kitto katsu* as a selling point in Japan.
7. **[T / F]** Japanese students think eating Kit Kats will bring good luck and help them pass their exams.

[🎧2-29]

Rocca: And to sell some not so mildly flavored Kit Kats to tourists.

Anyone ₆(   ) for a purple sweet potato

45　Kit Kat? Umm … Or a bite of a refreshing apple Kit Kat?

　　You'd say, a Kit Kat a day ₇(　　　　　　　　　).

Rocca: Woo! (reacts to *wasabi* taste)

50　Or perhaps you'd like to spice things up with a *wasabi* Kit Kat?

　　Hey, buddy, go easy on that sake Kit Kat!

　　It really does taste like sake.

55　**Lacroix:** We ₈(　　　　　　　) to foreigners because they have read in … on Facebook or social media that the Japanese Kit Kat was fantastic. So, when they come here, they wanna taste …

Rocca: … Kit Kat diplomacy.　(inaudible)

60　**Lacroix:** "United Color [sic]" of Kit Kat!

Comprehension Check

8. [T / F] The reporter uses a famous English proverb about apples and a popular expression about drinking too much alcohol to describe the unique flavors of Japanese Kit Kats.

9. [T / F] "United Colors of Kit Kat" means that Japanese Kit Kat candy bars have many flavors that appeal to many kinds of people.

10. [T / F] Tourists coming to Japan are eager to try Japanese Kit Kats because they have heard about them from TV commercials and magazines.

[CD 2-30]

Rocca: Back in his patisserie, chef Takagi indulged me, as we **went about** creating a new premium Kit Kat.

65　**Chef Takagi:** Raspberry, pistachio, strawberry.

---

refreshing apple
さわやかなリンゴ味の

spice ~ up
~にスパイスを加えてピリッとさせる

go easy on ~
~は控えめにね

diplomacy
外交

United Color(s) of ~
Benetton社のスローガンをもじったもの

patisserie
スイーツ店

indulged me
私がやりたいようにさせてくれた

pistachio
地中海沿岸で取れるナッツだがその緑色を活かして、ペーストにして製菓材料に用いることがある

Rocca: I know it ₉(   ), but could we mix the pistachio with the raspberry?

Takagi/Rocca (voiceover/translation): Shall we give that a try?

70 *Takagi/Rocca (voiceover/translation):* The color will probably be ghastly, but it smells good, doesn't it?

ghastly 不気味な

Takagi/Rocca (voiceover/translation): The color is awful, isn't it? Try a taste.

Rocca: It's very good!

75 *Chef Takagi:* Very good?

Rocca: It's very good! Try it!

Chef Takagi: Umm. Very good! *Oishii*!

Rocca: *Oishii*?

Chef Takagi: *Oishii*!

80 *Rocca:* *Oishii*. That means delicious. Behold … the Raspacchio Kit Kat! I believe I have ₁₀(   ).

Behold 見よ！

Chef Takagi: *Kitto kachimasu*. (I'm sure you will win.)

Rocca: *Kitto Katsu*. I got a *Kitto Katsu*! (I got a win!)

Comprehension Check

11. **[T / F]** Chef Takagi thought the reporter's suggestion to mix the pistachio and raspberry flavors would make a pretty color, but smell bad.

12. **[T / F]** The reporter got a win (*kitto katsu*) because Chef Takagi said the Raspacchio Kit Kat was delicious.

⑤ Summary

 2-31

Fill in the blanks. The first two letters of each word are already given.

Premium Kit Kat ₁(**co**   ) made in Japan are luxurious and more expensive than those made in America. The ₂(**ma**   ) behind these confections is pastry chef Yasumasa Takagi. He says Japanese prefer mild flavors more than ₃(**ag**   ) ones. The Japanese pronunciation of Kit Kat is similar to *kitto katsu*, which in Japanese means, "You surely will win!" Kit Kat candy is popular with Japanese students because they believe it is a ₄(**ta**   ) that will help them pass their exams. The company shrewdly decided to ₅(**ca**   ) on that. Kit Kat's Japan manager said Kit Kat's mission is to ₆(**en**   ) people. Tourists coming to Japan are eager to try Japanese Kit Kat bars because they have read about them on Facebook and social ₇(**me**   ). The reporter suggested mixing the pistachio and raspberry flavors together, and Chef Takagi gave it a ₈(**tr**   ). The reporter got a win (*kitto katsu*) because Chef Takagi said the Raspacchio Kit Kat was delicious (*oishii*).

   5

   10

⑥ Conversation in Action

 2-32

Put the Japanese statements into English. Then listen to check your answers.

Emma: Hey Jacob. **Have a Break, Have a Kit Kat*.

Jacob: Hey, thanks, Emma. Perfect timing!

Emma: You know, Kit Kats are different in Japan. And they're so popular. Like an obsession.

Jacob: It's because the ₁_____ of Kit Kat.　（その会社がその日本語の発音をうまく利用した）　*Kitto Katsu* means, "You will surely win!" So it's ₂_____.

　　　　　　　　　　（一種の食べられるお守り）

Emma: Huh. Whoever masterminded that concept is a genius. I thought it was because of the unique yummy flavors.

Jacob: That too. My friends say ₃_____.

　　　　　　　　　　（それらは味がマイルドで強くない）

Emma: Well, break time is over. Back to work!

Word Help *"Have a Break, Have a Kit Kat"* is the official worldwide tagline for Kit Kat.

7 Conversation in Action ⚠ CHALLENGE

Use the vocabulary and phrases you learned in Word Match and the news report scripts to make a short conversation with your partner. Then practice your conversation with your partner or group.

_____: _____
(Name)

_____: _____
(Name)

_____: _____
(Name)

_____: _____
(Name)

7 Critical Thinking

Discuss the following questions with your partner or group. Give reasons to support your opinions.

Understanding the News

1. How are Japanese Kit Kats different from those made in America?
2. Why are Kit Kats so popular in Japan?
3. Why do Japanese Kit Kats appeal to foreign tourists?

What Would You Do?

1. Did you know Kit Kat flavors in Japan are different from those in America? What are some other differences between Japanese sweets, foods, and beverages and those made outside Japan?
2. Do you like Kit Kat bars? Why? If not, what is your favorite candy? Why?
3. The reporter suggested mixing pistachio and raspberry flavors together to make a new flavor Kit Kat. What is your idea for a new Kit Kat flavor? Do you think people would like it? Discuss your answer with your partner or group.
4. Do you have a good luck charm? If so, what is it? Why do you believe it brings you good luck?

13 Mindfulness: Schools in England Teach Students to Relax

UNIT

Mental Health / Education

① Before You Watch

Look at the title and photos and then answer the questions.

1. What do you think the word, "mindfulness" means?

2. Why do you think England's schools are teaching students to relax?

2 Word Match

Match each word or phrase with its definition below.

( ) **1.** New research suggests that **mindfulness** meditation can help relieve pain and stress, and improve memory.

( ) **2.** He was very shy at first, but he gradually **open**ed **up** to his classmates.

( ) **3.** This recession has created tremendous **anxiety**, especially for young people.

( ) **4.** The countries of the world need to **tackle** the problem of climate change together.

( ) **5.** Diseases are **diagnose**d by medical tests and patient symptoms.

( ) **6.** Regular exercise is **beneficial** to your health.

( ) **7.** I didn't think I'd like that movie, but it **turn**ed **out to be** pretty good.

( ) **8.** The IT support team **conclude**d that a system update was required.

---

a. to become less shy and more willing to talk about your personal feelings and experiences

b. to deal with (something difficult)

c. to be discovered to be; to prove to be

d. producing good or helpful results or effects

e. a technique to help you relax by focusing on the present moment while accepting any thoughts and feelings without judgment

f. to decide (something) after a period of thought or research

g. a worried feeling you have because you think something bad might happen

h. to identify an illness or other problems by examining the symptoms

---

3 Getting the Gist (First Viewing) [Time 03:21]

Watch the news and choose the right word in each statement.

1. Stress-reducing exercises in mindfulness are (continuing / growing / lasting) in popularity around the world.

2. Researchers want to know if mindfulness exercises can (benefit / expand / produce) the mental health of children in England, where anxiety among kids is increasing.

4 Getting into Details (Second Viewing) [Time 03:21]

Watch or listen to the news again. Fill in the blanks and answer the questions.

[🎧2-34]

Anthony Mason: In our School Matters series, stress-reducing exercises in **mindfulness** are ₁(   ) across the world. Apps like Headspace and Calm have

5   more than 100 million users combined. Roxana Saberi takes a look at a one-of-a-kind study in England, giving students an education ₂(   ).

one-of-a-kind
ユニークな、独自の

10 **Female teacher:** Like feeling depressed … uh … actually scared … worried …

Roxana Saberi: At Arnold Academy, north of London, students are learning to **open up** …

Student #1: My great auntie died at the weekend.

15 **Saberi:** … about their **anxieties**.

Student #2: Um. I'm feeling a bit worried because my grandma has high blood pressure.

Student #3: Worried, because um, I get camera fright sometimes, and there's a camera pointing in my face right now.

camera fright
カメラ恐怖症

20 **Saberi:** Their list of concerns ₃(   ).

Student #4: There's so much work to do.

Student #5: I have lots of homework.

Olivia: My parents … Well, like kids
25   … They don't have, like, as much, like technology and social media. There's a lot of

pressure on that.

Comprehension Check

1. [T / F] New apps like Headspace and Calm are popular around the world.
2. [T / F] A unique study on whether mindfulness exercises can help students relax has started in America.
3. [T / F] The students at Arnold Academy are learning to be less shy about expressing their anxieties and personal problems in front of their teachers and other students.
4. [T / F] Olivia says parents have less pressure from technology and social media than kids do.

[🎧 2-35]

Saberi: To **tackle** these tensions, their school and nearly 400 others across England are trying $_4$( )...

30 *Male teacher:* Today's relaxation technique is called "Wings to the Sky."

Saberi: ... short, daily doses of relaxation ...

daily doses of ~
１日分の〜の用量

Male teacher: And as your arms are
35 falling, you can feel your stress leaving you.

Saberi: ... and mindfulness.

Saberi: Over three years, researchers plan to study whether exercises like these $_5$( ) the mental
40 health of children in England, where anxiety among kids is rising.

The trend is similar in the U.S. A recent survey found a 20 percent jump in American children **diagnose**d with anxiety over five years.

Comprehension Check

5. [T / F] The new study includes 400 students from across England.

6. [T / F] Anxiety among school children in England is increasing.

7. [T / F] A recent survey found that compared to England, the number of American children who have anxiety is decreasing.

[2-36]

45   *Professor Jessica Deighton:* If we find actually, you know, this is **beneficial**, then that's great.

Saberi: Professor Jessica Deighton says the government-backed trial in

50   England, which she's leading, is the largest of its kind.

government-backed trial
政府の支援を受けた試験的な取り組み

Prof. Deighton: In the early piloting, what they were saying was, ₆(   ), very busy, maybe busier than it was when we were children, and … uh … they find it's an opportunity to sit ... and reset.

piloting
実験的な試行

55   *Saberi:* That's why, history teacher Rachel Bradford says, after just two and a half months of these exercises, Arnold Academy saw an 80 percent drop in reports of misconduct.

misconduct
非行

Rachel Bradford: Now, they are able to calm down, and rationalize the situation.

rationalize the situation
状況を合理的に考える

60   *Harrison:* It just released my stress and stuff, and it's just helped me out a lot.

Saberi: How many of you feel that learning relaxation ₇(   )?

65   Olivia, you are not raising your hand.

Olivia: Right. My usual way of like, calming down is to move. So, that's why I do dance. When

70 you do, like, relaxation and breathing, it's like the complete
opposite. So, I don't really feel it.

8. [T / F] The mindfulness pilot study in England is the largest, and is supported by the government.

9. [T / F] Early results of the trial study show that children say the mindfulness exercises give them a chance to reset, calm down, and think about their problems more clearly.

10. [T / F] The mindfulness exercises are not effective because the number of misbehavior reports at Arnold Academy has increased.

11. [T / F] Olivia likes doing mindfulness exercises because they help improve her dancing.

[🎧 2-37]

Deighton: I think there's a danger that people get very carried away with one particular approach. I would say that's why it's really important to $_8($　　　　　　　), because actually this practice may **turn out** not **to be** effective.

> **get very carried away with ~**
> とても興奮して夢中になる

75 **Female teacher:** And you're gonna stretch up and try and catch the balloon.

Saberi: If researchers **conclude** that these practices are effective, supporters hope all schools in England will eventually offer them.

80 **Bradford:** Schools are not just there … to get children the best grades that they can. We're also here to help our children $_9($　　　　　　　)

85 versions of themselves.

Male teacher: And feel that stress leaving you …

Saberi: For CBS This Morning, Roxane Saberi, Bedford, England.

Comprehension Check

12. **[T / F]** Professor Jessica Deighton says doing mindfulness research is important because focusing on just one relaxation approach or technique may not be useful for everyone.

13. **[T / F]** Supporters of the research are not hopeful that mindfulness exercises can someday be used in every school in England.

14. **[T / F]** Going to school is not only about getting good grades. It's also about improving yourself and becoming the best person you can be.

5 Summary

 2-38

Fill in the blanks. The first two letters of each word are already given.

Stress-reducing exercises in ₁(**mi**   ) are gaining popularity across the world. In a one-of-a-kind government-backed trial, researchers plan to study whether mindfulness exercises can improve the ₂(**me**   ) health of children in England, where ₃(**an**   ) among kids is on the rise. A recent survey also found a 20 percent jump in American children 5 ₄(**di**   ) with anxiety. Early piloting shows the mindfulness exercises give children a chance to ₅(**ta**   ) their concerns by helping them open up, reset, calm down, and rationalize the situation. After two and a half months of these exercises, reports of misconduct at Arnold Academy ₆(**dr**   ) by 80 percent. The leader of the research trial 10 says this study is important because people should not think there is only one approach to solving the problem of anxiety among children. However, if researchers conclude that these exercises are ₇(**be**   ), supporters of the research hope all schools in England will eventually offer them. Going to school is not only about getting good ₈(**gr**   ). It's also about 15 improving yourself and becoming the best person you can be.

6 Conversation in Action

 2-39

Put the Japanese statements into English. Then listen to check your answers.

(Cellphone ringing …)

Jacob: Hey, Emma, what's up?

Emma: Hey, Jacob. I just finished another *Zoom class*. So now I'm gonna do a mindfulness exercise.

Jacob: Mindfulness? What's that?

Emma: Umm. It's a 1_____

so you can relax and relieve stress. （今のこの瞬間にただ集中して頭をすっきりさせる方法）

Jacob: Sounds really beneficial. Everyone can use that right now with the coronavirus *pandemic* and having to *quarantine*.

Emma: Staying at home and doing *social distancing* are really hard. It turns out

2_____.

（多くの人たちが不安症として診断されてきている）

Jacob: Maybe mindfulness exercises could 3_____

_____ to others who can help. （彼らが自分たちの心配事に立ち向かい心を開くのに役立つ）

Emma: They sure could! Hey, why don't you try it? I can text you one.

Jacob: Thanks, I will. Well, take care, and stay safe!

Word Help *Zoom class:* an online class in which everyone logs in to a web-conferencing system such as Zoom

pandemic: a disease that has spread over several countries / continents, affecting a large number of people

quarantine: separating and restricting the movement of people exposed (or potentially exposed) to a contagious disease

social distancing, physical distancing: maintaining a distance of 6 feet (2 meters) between people to help stop the spread of disease, including working from home, closing offices and schools, canceling events, and avoiding public transportation

---

7 Conversation in Action ⚠ CHALLENGE

Use the vocabulary and phrases you learned in Word Match and the news report scripts to make a short conversation with your partner. Then practice your conversation with your partner or group.

_____: _____
(Name)

_____: _____
(Name)

_____: _____
(Name)

_____: _____
(Name)

8 Critical Thinking

Discuss the following questions with your partner or group. Give reasons to support your opinions.

Understanding the News

1. What is mindfulness?

2. Why are researchers studying the effect of mindfulness exercises on school children in England?

3. What do the school children in the study say about the effects of the mindfulness exercises?

What Would You Do?

1. Have you ever heard of mindfulness? Would you like to try it? Why? / Why not?

2. Do you think mindfulness should be taught in schools in your country? Why? / Why not?

3. How do you deal with anxiety, stress, or a personal problem or a difficult situation? Would you recommend your strategy to others?

1 Before You Watch

Look at the title and photos and then answer the questions.

1. What is cursive writing?

2. Look at the picture with the cursive writing. Can you read any of the words?

2 Word Match

Match each word or phrase with its definition below.

( ) **1.** Plans are **under way** to build a new city hospital in the downtown area.

( ) **2.** I'm sure you will **get used to** our corporate culture after a while.

( ) **3.** People of all ages enjoy **the thrill of** seeing a celebrity in person.

( ) **4.** My niece **came up with** a solution to the puzzle.

( ) **5.** He's responsible for **oversee**ing the various stages of the project.

( ) **6.** We've only just met, but we **hit it off** straight away.

( ) **7.** It **turn**s **out** that our efforts to practice physical distancing have finally paid off.

( ) **8.** Always use a formal tone when writing to business **correspondent**s.

---

a. to watch somebody or something and make sure that a job or an activity is done correctly

b. to happen in a particular way, or to have a particular result

c. to have a good friendly relationship with somebody

d. to find or produce an answer to a problem

e. a person who writes letters, emails, etc. to another person regularly

f. happening now

g. to be familiar with something so that it seems normal or usual

h. feeling very excited or happy about something

---

3 Getting the Gist (First Viewing) [Time 04:02]

Watch the news and choose the right word in each statement.

1. For today's younger generation, cursive letters are hard to read. A handwriting revival in American schools is growing, and a new program is (guiding / learning / teaching) kids cursive handwriting.

2. Third graders at Good Shepherd Episcopal in Dallas are learning cursive by writing (emails / letters / texts) to their pen pals.

4 **Getting into Details (Second Viewing)** [Time 04:02]   2-41~45

Watch or listen to the news again. Fill in the blanks and answer the questions.

[2-41]

Reena Ninan: We end tonight on a handwritten note. Some of
America's most important historical documents go
back to the Declaration of
Independence – they're

5   in cursive. But for many
American school kids,
the curly letters are as
unreadable as ancient
hieroglyphics. In a growing number of states, a
10      $_1$(   ) is **under way**. Omar Villafranca,
now on the push to get Dallas kids ... in the loop.

Karen Gunter (teacher): This is the end of the thought.

Omar Villafranca: These third graders at Good Shepherd Episcopal
in Dallas are learning a $_2$(   ). They're
15   practicing cursive by writing letters to their pen pals.

Student: My third-grade teacher taught me cursive writing.

Villafranca: It's almost a $_3$(   ) for today's
younger generation.

Ahan Jain: It used to hurt my hand a lot, but now I **got used to** it.

20 *Villafranca:* Hard to read – and harder to write.

note
（短めの）手紙

Declaration of Independence
アメリカ独立宣言

ancient hieroglyphics
古代の象形文字

on the push to get ~ in the loop
～を同じ事をする仲間に引き入れようとする動きについて
loops & tailsには「ペン習字」の意味がありここではかけことばになっている

Comprehension Check

1. **[T / F]** Some of the most important documents in American history are written in cursive, but many American school children can't read or write it.
2. **[T / F]** For many American school kids, reading cursive might seem like trying to read ancient Egyptian writing.
3. **[T / F]** An increasing number of states have decided to discontinue teaching cursive.
4. **[T / F]** Learning cursive is part of the foreign language study program at Good Shepherd Episcopal School.
5. **[T / F]** Ahan Jain said writing in cursive hurt his hand at first because he was not used to it.

[CD 2-42]

Villafranca: Tim Mallad's daughter is in the class.

Tim Mallad: Wouldn't it be fun for the children ... to begin to learn ₄( ) and perhaps get **the thrill of** get**ting** a real letter in the mail?

in the mail
郵便で

25

Gunter: First thing we're going to do is look at the letter that is up on the screen.

30 *Villafranca:* He **came up with** the pen pal idea and shared it with her teacher, Karen Gunter.

Gunter: You got a letter today!

Male student: Another one?

Gunter: You got another one!

35 *Villafranca:* After he sent a letter – in cursive – to his daughter away at camp, and she couldn't read a word he had written.

away at camp
遠く離れたキャンプ
場にいる

Mallad: So she was mad at me. "Well, why are you mad at me?" "We ... your letter." And I'm thinking, I didn't say anything bad in the letter. "No, you wrote it in ₅( )."

40

Comprehension Check

6. [T / F] Tim Mallad got the pen pal idea from his daughter's teacher.
7. [T / F] Mallad sent a letter to his daughter at camp, but she couldn't read it because he wrote it in cursive.

[CD 2-43]

Villafranca: Mallad **oversee**s several retirement homes and knows a lot of people who still use that "funny writing." So he helped pair up students with several seniors, like 75-year-old Sue Standlee.

retirement homes
老人ホーム

103

45 *Sue Standlee:* It's difficult for me to ... to do text and emails, um ... or text, anyway, because there's so many shortened, abbreviated things that I
50 don't know what they are.

abbreviated
省略された

Gunter: Don't forget the dates at the top of your pages, please.

Villafranca: Sue was matched up with nine-year-old Samantha Moseley, and the pair instantly **hit it off** on paper.

was matched up with ~
～とペアになった

Samantha Moseley: I feel like I'm actually
55 talking to her. This has made me like, $_6($
) a lot more.

Gunter: This is excellent, excellent penmanship!

penmanship
筆記体の英習字

60 *Villafranca:* Third-grade teacher Karen Gunter says the cursive lesson also allows her to teach grammar along with the mechanics of writing.

Gunter: What does a capital D look like?

Villafranca: And it's one of the only times she knows the students
65 are $_7($).

mechanics of writing
文を書くときの決まり事（スペリング、大文字小文字の区別、句読法など）

Gunter: When we're writing the letters, they are quiet.

Villafranca: But during other times in class?

Gunter: Oh, no. They ...

Villafranca: It's mayhem.

mayhem
大騒ぎ

70 *Gunter:* Some of them never shut up. (laughing)

8. [T / F] Mallad made a pen pal list by matching seniors at retirement homes with kids in his daughter's class.

9. [T / F] Sue Standlee said that it was easier to text and send emails than write letters.

10. [T / F] Third-grade teacher Karen Gunter said she uses the cursive lessons to teach grammar and the rules of written language, such as capitalization, punctuation, and spelling.

11. [T / F] Gunter says her students talk too much and don't pay attention during the cursive lessons.

[🔊2-44]

Villafranca: 80-year-old retired writer Nancy Miller was worried she wouldn't have anything $_8$(   ) with her nine-year-old pen pal, Ahan Jain.

Nancy Miller: And in the very first
75   paragraph or two, he says, "I'm a Dallas Cowboys' fan and my favorite player is Dez Bryant." And I thought, "Wow, we $_9$(

80   ) right away."

Villafranca: **Turns out** Nancy and Ahan both have strong opinions on their beloved Dallas Cowboys.

So what are you writing to her about now?

Ahan: Brandon Marshall got cut and now Dez is gonna sign with
85   the Giants.

Villafranca: Is this better than text messaging? Is this better than emails?

Ahan: Yes.

Villafranca: How come?

90 *Ahan:* Because in text messaging, you don't have a visual of the

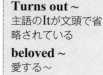

Turns out ~
主語のItが文頭で省略されている

beloved ~
愛する~

got cut
チームから外された

have a visual of the person
その人がどんな人か心に思い浮かべる

person, but in the letters, you do.

12. [T / F] At first, Nancy Miller was afraid that she would not be able to find anything in common with her new pen pal.

13. [T / F] Ahan Jain says writing letters is better than text messaging because it helps you get a visual image of the person.

[🎵 2-45]

Villafranca: After a few months exchanging letters, the students finally got a ₁₀(   ) their cursive

95   **correspondent**.

Standlee: Oh, I'm so glad to meet you!

Villafranca: Sue and Samantha are now more than pen pals.

Standlee: Oh, she's just flamboyant. She's a pistol. She's ... You have beautiful blue eyes.

100 *Samantha:* Thank you.

Standlee: It was wonderful to meet her, just wonderful.

Samantha: I got to meet someone new and not just writing to them in short letters and stuff, I
105   actually ₁₁(   ) with her.

Villafranca: In a world of constant emails, texts, and direct messages, the kids say, there's nothing like that "funny writing" to ₁₂(   ). Omar Villafranca,
110   CBS News, Dallas.

flamboyant
華やかな、かわい
らしい
pistol
活動的で元気な子

got to ~
~する機会を得た、
~できた
~ and stuff
~など

14. [T / F] Sue Standlee thinks Samantha has a very lively and creative personality.

15. [T / F] Samantha Moseley was disappointed because she didn't think she and Sue Standlee would become friends.

5 Summary

 2-46

Fill in the blanks. The first two letters of each word are already given.

Some of the most important documents in American history are written in
₁(**cu**   ), but many American school children can't read or
write it. Now a handwriting ₂(**re**   ) is growing in many states.
Tim Mallad ₃(**ca**   ) up with the idea of helping children to
learn cursive by writing to a pen pal. He thought they would also get the   5
₄(**th**   ) of receiving a letter in the mail. He shared his pen pal
idea with his daughter's teacher. Mallad oversees several retirement homes,
so he helped ₅(**pa**   ) up the students with seniors. One of the
kids said writing in cursive used to hurt his hand at first, but he got used to it
and came to like it. Nancy Miller was worried she would not be able to find   10
anything to write about to her new pen pal. However, it ₆(**tu**   )
out that the seniors and students hit it ₇(**of**   ), and they all
began to share their opinions in cursive writing. After a few months of
exchanging letters, the students met their ₈(**co**   ). The children
were happy to get to meet and make new friends.   15

6 Conversation in Action

 2-47

Put the Japanese statements into English. Then listen to check your answers.

Jacob: What are you doing, Emma?

Emma: I'm writing a letter to my grandma in New York.

Jacob: Writing a letter! Wow, not many people do that nowadays.

Emma: I know. It's difficult for her to do text messaging or email. I never learned
cursive, so it was ₁_____
_____. (最初は読んだり書いたりするのが難しいけど、慣れたわ)

Jacob: She must really ₂_____. Who came
up with the idea?   (君から便りをもらってわくわくする)

Emma: My mom did. It's great because it keeps us ₃_____
_____. (なぜかと言うとそれで私たちはつながりを持てて、私は
彼女のことをもっとよく知ることもできるから)

Jacob: I have a grandmother in Oregon. I'll ask if she wants to try it.

Emma: Let me know how that turns out. Hey, Jacob, I can teach you cursive!

Jacob: Ha, sounds good. See you!

7 Conversation in Action | ⚠ CHALLENGE

Use the vocabulary and phrases you learned in Word Match and the news report scripts to make a short conversation with your partner. Then practice your conversation with your partner or group.

_____: _____
(Name)

_____: _____
(Name)

_____: _____
(Name)

_____: _____
(Name)

8 Critical Thinking

Discuss the following questions with your partner or group. Give reasons to support your opinions.

Understanding the News

1. How did Tim Mallad come up with the idea for students to write letters to seniors?

2. What did the children's third-grade teacher say was a benefit of her cursive lessons?

3. Did the students enjoy learning cursive and meeting their pen pals? Why?

What Would You Do?

1. Why do you think people nowadays can't read or write cursive? Do you think it's important to be able to read and write cursive? Why?/Why not?

2. Can you read and write cursive? If not, would you like to learn it? Why?/ Why not?

3. Imagine you have a new pen pal. Write a brief letter about youtself in cursive. Include topics like hobbies, sports or music you like, etc. Was writing the letter in cursive easy or difficult? Why? Discuss your letter with your partner or group.

15 The Great Train Race: Rail Service in Japan and the U.S.

UNIT

Lifestyle / Culture

1 Before You Watch

Look at the title and photos and then answer the questions.

1. Which country do you think has better train service, America or Japan?

2. Which country do you think has faster high-speed train service, America or Japan?

2 Word Match

Match each word or phrase with its definition below.

(   ) **1.** Jason was always **on the move**, never staying in one place for more than a few days.

(   ) **2.** Many people who started working from home because of the pandemic now say that their daily **commute** was a huge waste of time.

(   ) **3.** It's such a **chore** to do the shopping every day.

(   ) **4.** We will begin **board**ing soon. Please make sure you have all your belongings and leave nothing behind.

(   ) **5.** This new data mining software will improve the **efficiency** of our research department.

(   ) **6.** Since you're a pro in this field, I **could use** your advice on this project.

(   ) **7.** What's the one-way bus **fare** to Osaka?

(   ) **8.** I'm **look**ing **forward to** working with you.

---

a. the quality of doing something well with no waste of time or money

b. the money that you pay to travel by bus, plane, taxi, etc.

c. to be thinking with pleasure about something that is going to happen

d. traveling to and from work or school every day

e. used to say that you would like to have something very much

f. to get on a ship, train, plane, bus, etc.

g. an unpleasant or boring task

h. traveling from one place to another; very active and busy

---

3 Getting the Gist (First Viewing) [Time 04:52]

Watch the news and choose the right word in each statement.

1. A team of CBS News correspondents traveled to Japan, Greece, Southern Africa and Scotland to (admire / learn / recognize) how and why people travel in those countries.

2. CBS This Morning Saturday co-anchor, Michelle Miller reported about a friendly (contest / gamble / game) between the U.S. and Japan to find out which country has better train service.

4 Getting into Details (Second Viewing) [Time 04:52] 🖥WEB動画 📀DVD 💿CD 2-49~53

Watch or listen to the news again. Fill in the blanks and answer the questions.

[💿 2-49]

Anthony Mason: This morning we're introducing a special four-part series called, World of Motion. A team of CBS News correspondents ₁( ) to Japan, Greece, Southern Africa, and Scotland, to discover how
5   and why people are **on the move**.

CBS This Morning Saturday co-anchor, Michelle Miller is here with the results of a
    ₂( )
    between the U.S. and Japan,
10 focusing on train travel.
    Michelle, good morning.

Michelle Miller: Good morning. The daily **commute** can be a **chore** no matter where you live. But some definitely have it
    ₃( ). My colleague,
15 Ramy Inocencio rode the rails in Japan, while I **board**ed trains right here to see how American ingenuity stacks up to Japanese **efficiency**.

ingenuity stacks up to ~
創意あふれる考案品が~に匹敵する

Comprehension Check

1. **[T / F]** CBS News correspondents in Japan, Greece, Southern Africa and Scotland are trying to find out how and why people move to these countries.
2. **[T / F]** The daily trip to work or school and back can be tedious wherever you live.
3. **[T / F]** To compare the rail service between Japan and America, Michelle Miller rode the rails in Japan, while Ramy Inocencio boarded trains in New York City.

[💿 2-50]

Miller: Rush hour in New York City is a daily challenge for its commuters who, like most Americans, tend to ₄(
20) as their main source of transportation.

This, despite the city having the nation's largest subway system, spanning more than 665 miles, carrying over

spanning ~
~にも渡って
665 miles
= 1070km

111

5.6 million passengers every year.

25 **Ramy Inocencio:** Crowds … They are a thing here in Tokyo too, Michelle. This city has a population of 14 million people, and about half of them take to the rails every day. And here's something that might be surprising to Americans: 30 people here ₅(

) for trains that arrive on time, nearly every time.

They are a thing ... too
ここ東京でも同じ（現象）です

Miller: Here at Times Square Station, New York's busiest, people here might be surprised to know there's a schedule at 35 all. As for lining up? Huh. Forget about it.

Inocencio: In Tokyo, stations aren't just places to ₆(

). They're also destinations to get a gourmet meal, like here, at Ramen Row.

Forget about it.
（Fuggedaboutit のように発音される）もうその事はいいわ、忘れて

Miller: The dining choices here aren't as good.

Comprehension Check

4. **[T / F]** New York City commuters, like most Americans, travel by car.
5. **[T / F]** America's largest subway system is in New York City.
6. **[T / F]** Tokyo trains carry about half the number of New York City's train passengers each day.
7. **[T / F]** The reporter says New Yorkers forget their train schedules, so they can't line up for trains like Japanese train riders do.
8. **[T / F]** Tokyo train stations do not have many restaurants where people can enjoy fine food.

[🎧 2-51]

40 **Inocencio:** *The Guinness Book of World Records* says Tokyo's Shinjuku Station is ₇(

).

Look how clean it is.

Miller: Sure, these trains and stations 45 **could use** a bit more attention, but despite all that and the delays, this subway runs 24 hours a day.

Inocencio: Subway service in Tokyo ends at around midnight, and restarts at around 5 a.m. That lets crews tend to station
50 maintenance.

Miller: No matter what time you ride, or how far the trip, the **fare** in New York is the same.

Inocencio: Prices here vary depending on how far you go. But it's
55 $_8($) that matters most to rail passengers in Japan. The bullet train, or the Shinkansen, is still the world's most reliable form of public transportation. We're boarding in Tokyo for a trip to Kyoto, 319 miles away.

crews
駅員

tend to ~
〜に気を配る

319 miles
= 513km

Comprehension Check

 9. [T / F] Tokyo's Shinjuku Station is the busiest in the world.
10. [T / F] Even though New York City's stations are not as clean as Tokyo's, the subway trains run all day and night.
11. [T / F] The train fare in New York changes according to the time of day and destination.
12. [T / F] Ramy Inocencio says Japanese train passengers care more about time than the cost of the fare.

[CD 2-52]
60 *Miller:* And we'll ride Amtrak's high-speed rail. The Acela, from New York to Washington, D.C., which is about 225 miles. $_9($) a nearly 100-mile head start!
65 Let's see who gets there first!

225 miles
= 362km

100-mile head start
最初から100マイル
(160km)有利なハ
ンディがある状態

Inocencio: Michelle, you did hear that bit about this being the world's most reliable high-speed train service ride. It's also super-fast, with a top speed of 177 miles per hour

177 miles
= 284km

on this line.

70 **Miller:** That is pretty fast, Ramy. The Acela only averages about 82 miles per hour. Part of the reason for that … it shares its tracks with both its ₁₀( ) and freight trains, too.

82 miles
= 131km

freight trains
貨物列車

Inocencio: Ah, well, that was pleasant. Here we are in Kyoto, 75 Michelle, right on time, an exact 2 hours and 18 minutes.

Miller: Congratulations, Ramy. If we stay on schedule, which Amtrak doesn't 20 percent of the time, we should get to D.C. in about … oh … 40 minutes … although … Amtrak is promising some upgrades. It should shave 80 15 minutes off of the commute by the year 2021. Fifteen whole minutes!

Amtrak
全米鉄道旅客輸送会社

shave ~ off of …
…から～を削減する

Inocencio: And that's something to **look forward to**, Michelle. In the meantime, with the extra time we've got now, we're 85 gonna ₁₁( ) to Japan's old imperial capital. Wish you were here!

THE GREAT TRAIN RACE

old imperial capital
皇都、帝都

Miller: Yeah, me too, Ramy. Me too. Nice kimono.

Comprehension Check

13. **[T / F]** The Acela's top speed is 82 miles per hour.
14. **[T / F]** The reason the Acela cannot go faster is because it shares tracks with local lines and freight trains.
15. **[T / F]** Forty percent of Acela trains do not run on time.
16. **[T / F]** Amtrack says some future upgrades should cut the commute time to Washington D.C. by 15 minutes.

[🎧 2-53]

Mason: (Laughter)

90 **Miller:** To recap, Ramy rode a train about 100 miles further [sic], and completed that trip roughly 40 minutes sooner

To recap
要点をまとめると
further
正しくはfartherと
なるべき

than I did. So, when it comes to traveling by train, Americans are ₁₂( ) our friends in Japan. But the Shinkansen may be making its way to the United States. There's a private company in Texas. They hope to start next year, between Dallas and Houston, shaving that, or trimming that ... that commute down to 90 minutes.

95

making its way to ~ ～にやってくる	
shaving カットして	

Comprehension Check

17. [T / F] Tokyo is farther from Kyoto than New York City is to Washington, D.C., so the Shinkansen train ride from Tokyo to Kyoto took longer.
18. [T / F] Miller says American rail service is superior to Japan's.
19. [T / F] A private company in Texas is planning to bring high-speed rail service like the Shinkansen to the United States.

5 Summary

🎧 2-54

Fill in the blanks. The first two letters of each word are already given.

Michelle Miller reported the results of a friendly ₁(**co**) between the U.S. and Japan, focusing on train travel. Miller's colleague, Ramy Inocencio, rode trains in Japan, while she boarded trains in New York City. New York City has the nation's largest ₂(**su**) system, spanning more than 665 miles, and carrying over 5.6 million passengers every year. About half of Tokyo's population of 14 million people ride trains daily. Like New York City, crowds are a thing in Tokyo. People politely ₃(**li**) up for trains that almost always arrive on schedule, which might be surprising to Americans. Shinjuku Station is the ₄(**bu**) in the world and is very clean. On the other hand, Times Square Station is the busiest in America, and even though it could be cleaner and trains are often ₅(**be**) schedule, the subway runs 24 hours a day, and the ₆(**fa**) is the same no matter what time or how far you ride. Japanese train passengers care more about ₇(**ti**) than the cost of the fare. Inocencio

5

10

15

boarded the Shinkansen in Tokyo for a trip to Kyoto, 319 miles away. The Shinkansen has a top speed of 177 miles per hour. Miller boarded The Acela from New York to Washington, D.C., which is about 225 miles away. The Acela averages about 82 miles per hour. The Shinkansen arrived in Kyoto right on $_8$(**ti**). Inocencio rode a train about 100 miles farther and completed that trip roughly 40 minutes $_9$(**so**) than Miller did. When it $_{10}$(**co**) to traveling by train, America is far behind Japan.

20

6 Conversation in Action

 2-55

Put the Japanese statements into English. Then listen to check your answers.

Announcement: The train will arrive soon. Please stand behind the yellow line.

Jacob: Well, we're finally on the move! Hurry, Emma, or $_1$_____. (僕ら列車に遅れちゃうよ)

Emma: OK, Jacob … I just want to get some *ekiben* for our trip.

Jacob: Eki what?

Emma: *Ekiben* … a station box lunch. It's a thing here. Oh, there's some over there!

Jacob: We $_2$_____, too. I'm so looking forward to riding the Shinkansen! My daily train commute is such a chore. (何か飲み物もあるといいね)

Emma: We got a really *good deal on the fare, too!

Jacob: And Kyoto is $_3$_____. (観光するにはすばらしい場所)

Emma: OK, I've got our *ekiben* and drinks. Here comes the train!

Jacob: Awesome! Let's go!

> **Word Help**   ***a good deal:** a bargain, or something bought at a cheap or low price   *Example:* She got a *good deal* on her new computer.

7 Conversation in Action  CHALLENGE

Use the vocabulary and phrases you learned in Word Match and the news report scripts to make a short conversation with your partner. Then practice your conversation with your partner or group.

_____: _____
(Name)

_____: _____
(Name)

_____: _____
(Name)

_____: _____
(Name)

8 Critical Thinking

Discuss the following questions with your partner or group. Give reasons to support your opinions.

Understanding the News

1. Why did a team of CBS News correspondents travel to Japan, Greece, Southern Africa, and Scotland?

2. How do most Americans commute?

3. What did the news reporters say are some differences between New York City and Tokyo regarding the rail services and daily commute?

4. What are some differences between Japan's Shinkansen and America's Acela high-speed trains?

What Would You Do?

1. Describe your daily commute. Include length of time, how you spend time on the train, experiences during rush hour, etc.

2. What do you think of the rail service in Japan? Discuss some things you like and dislike. Why? What would you suggest to improve it?

3. Describe the rail service in a country you have visited, or a memorable train trip in Japan. Include comments about train fare, speed, efficiency, cleanliness, comfort, convenience, etc.

Web動画のご案内　***StreamLine***

本テキストの映像は、オンラインでのストリーミング再生になります。下記URLよりご利用ください。なお**有効期限は、はじめてログインした時点から1年半**です。

http://st.seibido.co.jp

1 ログイン画面

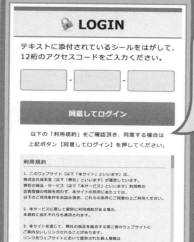

🔒 **LOGIN**

テキストに添付されているシールをはがして、12桁のアクセスコードをご入力ください。

[　　] - [　　] - [　　]

同意してログイン

以下の「利用規約」をご確認頂き、同意する場合は上記ボタン【同意してログイン】を押してください。

利用規約

巻末に添付されているシールをはがして、アクセスコードをご入力ください。

2 メニュー画面

AFP World Focus
—Environment, Health, and Technology—
アクセスコード有効期限：2018年4月30日

🎬 **Video**　　🎵 **Audio**

Lesson 1: Global Warming and Climat... ＞
Lesson 2: Diet and Health for Long ... ＞
Lesson 3: Self-Driving for the Futu... ＞
Lesson 4: Sustaining Biodiversity a... ＞
Lesson 5: 3D Printers for Creating ... ＞
Lesson 6: IT and Education ＞
Lesson 7: Protection from Natural D... ＞
Lesson 8: Practical Uses of Drones ... ＞

「Video」または「Audio」を選択すると、それぞれストリーミング再生ができます。

3 再生画面

AFP World Focus
—Environment, Health, and Technology—
アクセスコード有効期限：2018年4月30日

Lesson 2:
Diet and Health for Long Lives
食習慣：長生きのためのスーパーフードを探す

推奨動作環境

【PC OS】
Windows 7~ ／ Mac 10.8~

【Mobile OS】
iOS ／ Android　※Androidの場合は4.x~が推奨

【Desktop ブラウザ】
Internet Explorer 9~ / Firefox / Chrome / Safari / Microsoft Edge

TEXT PRODUCTION STAFF

edited by 編集
Minako Hagiwara 萩原 美奈子
Takashi Kudo 工藤 隆志

cover design by 表紙デザイン
Nobuyoshi Fujino 藤野 伸芳

text design by 本文デザイン
Ruben Frosali ルーベン・フロサリ

illustration by イラスト
Yoko Sekine 関根 庸子

CD PRODUCTION STAFF

recorded by 吹き込み者
Rachel Walzer (AmE) レイチェル・ワルザー（アメリカ英語）
Jack Merluzzi (AmE) ジャック・マルージ（アメリカ英語）

CBS NewsBreak 5
CBSニュースブレイク 5

2021年1月20日　初版発行
2023年3月10日　第6刷発行

編著者　熊井 信弘　Stephen Timson

発行者　佐野 英一郎

発行所　株式会社 成美堂
〒101-0052　東京都千代田区神田小川町3-22
TEL 03-3291-2261　FAX 03-3293-5490
https://www.seibido.co.jp

印刷・製本　三美印刷(株)

ISBN 978-4-7919-7230-2　　　　　　　　Printed in Japan